THE
AMERICAN INDIAN
GHOST DANCE,
1870 and 1890

**Recent Titles in
Bibliographies and Indexes in American History**

THE AMERICAN INDIAN GHOST DANCE, 1870 and 1890

An Annotated Bibliography

COMPILED BY
SHELLEY ANNE OSTERREICH

Bibliographies and Indexes in American History,
Number 19

GREENWOOD PRESS
New York • Westport, Connecticut • London

Library of Congress Cataloging-in-Publication Data

Osterreich, Shelley Anne.
    The American Indian ghost dance, 1870 and 1890 : an annotated
bibliography / compiled by Shelley Anne Osterreich.
        p.   cm.—(Bibliographies and indexes in American history,
    ISSN 0742-6828 ; no. 19)
    Includes indexes.
    ISBN 0-313-27469-X (alk. paper)
    1. Ghost dance—Bibliography. 2. Indians of North America—Great
Plains—Dances—Bibliography. 3. Indians of North America—Great
Plains—Religion and mythology—Bibliography. 4. Indians of North
America—Great Plains—History—19th century—Bibliography.
    I. Title. II. Series.
Z1209.2.U52G757   1991
[E98.D2]
016.978′00497—dc20   91-7957

British Library Cataloguing in Publication Data is available.

Library of Congress Catalog Card Number: 91-7957
ISBN: 0-313-27469-X
ISSN: 0742-6828

First published in 1991

Greenwood Press, 88 Post Road West, Westport, CT   06881
An imprint of Greenwood Publishing Group, Inc.

Printed in the United States of America

The paper used in this book complies with the
Permanent Paper Standard issued by the National
Information Standards Organization (Z39.48-1984).

10 9 8 7 6 5 4 3 2 1

To Norbert,

Shaianne and Airisenne

Contents

Acknowledgments

I have assembled this bibliography in the hope of revealing some of the topics or paths of inquiry into the Ghost Dance which have been pursued by previous scholars. The annotations should suggest various lines of inquiry helpful to investigators generally concerned with the history and/or anthropology connected with this topic. I am extremely grateful to the authors included in this work, for their curiosity, and for their pursuit of these topics for which we share a common intrigue.

In addition to the many years of personal friendship shared with Dr. Michael Hittman, chairman of Anthropology and Sociology at the Zeckendorf Campus of Long Island University in Brooklyn, New York, I have been graced by the benefits of the enthusiasm and generosity he has shown me concerning his own plentiful investigations into issues pertaining to the Ghost Dance Movements. This is particularly so in relation to the work he has done concerning the very central personality of the Ghost Dance Movement of 1890, namely, Wovoka, the prophet-messiah of this Ghost Dance. In a very large part, it was from conversations and correspondence with Dr. Hittman that I became involved with the Indian Ghost Dance. His guidance through his own extensively gathered bibliography concerning this subject has been invaluable. It is therefore to this kind friend and scholar that I am in the greatest debt.

I must likewise thank the limitless patience and cooperation of my colleagues, June Welwood, Steve Cauffman and Kiyomi Galouskas in the inter-library loan facility in the Elihu Burritt Library at Central Connecticut State University. Without their enthusiastic participation in this project, I would soon have arrived at a genuine impasse. On the technical end of the matter, my relativley short computer skills were assisted in great measure by John Rutherford. I am also very thankful for the assistance I received in the Faculty Computer Center at Central. I must further thank my immediate colleagues and my supervisor, Priya Rai in the Technical Processing Department, for guidance, support and ultimately, indulgence. Finally, I am grateful for the generous amounts of professional leave awarded to me by my colleagues within the library and the University's administration. Without this allotted freedom, the effort to produce this bibliography would never have been possible.

Introduction

In late December of 1890, a small band of Miniconjous Sioux fled the reservation at Pine Ridge Agency in South Dakota, trying to escape into the Bad Lands, or maybe to Canada. A massive congregation of Indians had collected at Pine Ridge, many for food, many (over 3,000) to dance the Ghost Dance. The Miniconjous band was eventually intercepted by one of the many U.S. cavalry units which had converged on the area, and they were escorted back to the Agency. They all stopped for the night on December 31, about twenty miles from the Agency. It was 44 degrees below freezing. The formal surrendering of arms had been arranged for the next morning. However mistrust, fear and tension along with a misplaced feeling of strength and invulnerability on the part of the Indians, possibly combined with the U.S. military's need for revenge, resulted in the immediate deaths of 146 Indian men, women and children, as well as 47 whites. This infamous event which occurred on the night of December 31, 1890 and the day of January 1, 1891 has subsequently been called the Wounded Knee Massacre.

This Ghost Dance, flourishing in 1888-1891 among the Indian tribes in the American west held a promise of hope: hope for a recognizable life and a continued satisfying relationship with the world as they had always known it to be. So many of them had died in wars with the whites, from disease carried by the white men, and also from starvation. This religion of the Ghost Dance promised that all the dead families and friends would return. It promised the white men would be gone. It promised the buffalo and all the other game would again roam the earth.

Life as it had been was no longer available to the Indians. The massive buffalo herds were all gone. With them, the major food supply, had also gone the primary source of clothing and shelter material, and even ceremonial religious objects. The land had been taken from them. The very idea of *owning the land* was still inconceivable to most Indians. What was not inconceivable to them was that the whites were crowding them onto smaller and smaller sections of land which were called *reservations*. The whites had prohibited them from practicing their religious ceremonies, and now the whites were insisting they move away from the tribe onto private farms. The Indians had no farming experience or equipment, and the land in South Dakota did not invite farming, even for experts.

The Ghost Dance idea that spread in the late 1880's was begun by a Paiute from Nevada by the name of Wovoka. Sometime in 1888, he fell into a trance, possibly like other religious experiences in his culture, but also possibly induced by scarlet fever, and possibly during a solar eclipse. In this trance, he saw 'heaven' and all his departed friends and relations. He spoke with the Great Father, who taught him a special dance and special songs. His mission from the Great Father was to teach this dance and these songs to *all* the Indians. If they would follow his instructions, in peace with each other <u>and</u> with the whites, the world would be renewed. The dead would return, the game would return and the whites would be gone. When Wovoka, also called Jack Wilson, awoke, he began this mission. It was not difficult. The Indians were out of options. This message of Wovoka's spread like mercury, in Nevada first, and then west to California and east to Wyoming, North and South Dakota, eventually into possibly 16 states. Part of the 'translation' of this message, from one tribe to another, was that Wovoka was the messiah. Part of the message, as carried to the destitute Sioux in the Dakotas was that the Indians could be responsible for the demise of the whites. The message, as it traveled through the many tribes, became altered to fit the needs of the individual people addressing it as a possible salvation. The Miniconjous warriors at Wounded Knee felt themselves to be invulnerable to the bullets of the whites, because they were wearing magic Ghost Dance Shirts, an innovation possibly introduced to the Sioux by Short Bull after his pilgrimage to Wovoka for instruction.

The impact of the encroachment of the white man had begun to take its toll decades before this Ghost Dance Movement in 1888. By 1869 in Nevada, the destruction done to the culture and livelihood to the Indians there had resulted in a similar impasse. The game had been practically decimated. Fish, the main food source for the Paiute tribe, had been nearly fished out of the lakes in that area. The reservation system had been put into place there also, sometimes resulting in the 'assignment' of tribes hostile to each other to the same reservation. In 1869, another Paiute, referred to as Wodziwob also had a 'dream.' His message was very similar to that of Wovoka. Initiating the <u>first</u> Ghost Dance in 1870, Wodziwob's message was that if the Indians danced the Ghost Dance, and followed all his instructions, the world would be renewed in the spring of 1871. This movement was also well received by many tribes. One of Wodziwob's apostles was a man called Tavibo, who was Wovoka's father.

Travel and communication was less advanced at this earlier time. Nevertheless, this movement spread throughout California and possibly to

Oregon or Washington. However, interest for many fell when the time for the renewal came and went, with no observable renewal.

Not all whites were uncaring or oblivious to the damage being done to these original North American inhabitants. Even while these events were occurring, records were being kept, and observations being made. For as long as possible, investigations were made through the original participants. However, even in 1933, when Cora DuBois was doing her field work in California on the 1870 Ghost Dance, she notes her informants are, necesarily 65 to 70 years old. Unable to change the past, many men and women have attempted to know exactly what it was that happened, and, even more difficult, to understand it. The Ghost Dance Movements of 1869-1872 and 1888-1891 have presented a fascination to historians and sociologists from the time they occurred.

I have attempted to include in this bibliography, a sample of the wide variety of the material available concerning both of these American Indian Ghost Dance Movements. Histories are available from the Indians, from the military, from the settlers, from newspaper reporters, and from subsequent historians. One of the first American ethnologists arrived on the scene of the Pine Ridge Agency days after the Wounded Knee Massacre: James Mooney. Mooney traveled throughout the area of Ghost Dance contact, and compiled a history of the movement. It is an encompasssing record and a timely report. Subsequent inquiries have frequently used his collection of observations, statements, and documents in the pursuit of further studies.

Subsequent to Mooney's investigation, the importance of the Ghost Dance of 1870 has come to light. Extensive field research revealed the spread of that Movement into California, where it lasted longer than elsewhere and took on several different forms, still recognizable but unique. This research also revealed the possible existence of aboriginal religious practice, possibly throughout California, Oregon, and Washington state, which contained many of the features of both the later movements.

The various branches of the social sciences have taken many avenues in their inquiry into the Ghost Dance. Terms to explain or to describe its necessity, its attraction, or its qualitites of fulfillment have emerged. The discussions revolve around movements of acculturation, nativistic movements, revitalization movements, revivalization movements, and messianic movements, among others.

The intention in collecting, annotating and offering this bibliographic collection is to provide access to a selection of the available material on these Ghost Dance Movements. The year 1990 marked the one hundredth anniversary of the tragedy at Wounded Knee Creek, which was provoked by the celebration of the Ghost Dance. Virtually all of the Ghost Dance participants are now dead. It is my hope that this publication will in some way contribute to an understanding of what the Ghost Dance was, what was its ultimate effect, and what we can learn from this period of cultural upheaval and intense suffering.

Please note the numbers following the entries in the indexes refer to page numbers, and not to annotations.

1
Ghost Dance Histories and Observations

1. Brown, Dee. *Bury My Heart at Wounded Knee : An Indian History of the American West.* New York : Bantam Books, 1972.

    An intimate and comprehensive account is presented of the conquest of the American West, of the destruction of the Indian culture and civilization, made from the oral history available through the participants' own words, through recorded treaties, formal meetings between U.S. government officials, civilians and various Indians and/or groups of Indians.

    Brown's use of "their own words" provides a moving picture of the Indian chiefs and warriors. He details Red Cloud, (the Ogala Sioux), Crazy Horse, (a younger Ogala), Sitting Bull (Tatanka Yotanka), and Dull Knife, (the Northern Cheyanne) to name just a few.

2. Fletcher, Alice C. "The Indian Messiah." *Journal of American Folklore* 4(12):55-57(1891).

    Fletcher offers a chronicle of the beginning of the 1890 Ghost Dance. It is said to have started with a young Cheyenne, living among the Arapaho. While in mourning, he fell into a trance, met several deceased friends, eventually met with a messiah, in a robe and with light skin, who claimed to be the Son of God. This messiah said the Indians should worship him and that he would restore the vanished herds of buffalo, and that there would be no more suffering from hunger; that "the dead would be reunited with the living." Others around him also began to "have visions, and began to hear songs." "Following the lines of other ancient Indian cults, the people fell in trances as they danced, and were supposed to talk with the dead and learn of the future life. From this simple beginning, the Ghost Dance grew." The major variations lay in the manner in which the "white race" would dissappear (e.g. earthquake, cyclone, landslide, etc.).

Fletcher describes the dance as understood from a Sioux delegation "visiting in Washington in February, 1891...." She reports "the songs sung at the dance were in the Arapaho tongue" and that the dance "resembled that of the 'Woman's Dance'." She further offers the following assertion: "The Ghost Dance presents nothing new as a rite, as it holds to old forms in the trance, the manner of dancing, and use of the pole. Its teachings of a deliverer, and the events to follow his coming are equally old. The belief in a deliverer can be traced as far back as we have any records of the aborigines. It is one of their fundamental myths." Here, Fletcher notes the conspicuous fact that the image of the messiah held by the Indians is the image of the God of their oppressors. She also quotes a group of Ogalala Sioux "argueing the superiority of the Indian's reverence and sacrifice in the Sun Dance over the cruelty and cowardice of the Christians, who were not only guilty, by their own account, of murdering God's son, but who sought to secure through this act their vicarious release from future suffering." There is no documentation attached to this article, no reference to any field work, no research implied.

Fletcher does recount the damage done to the aboriginal life of the Indians, the elimination of their food source, and their relocation onto reservations. However, she concludes by saying, "It is not unlikely that the [Ghost Dance] craze would have died out without any serious trouble, having been overcome by the quiet, persistent influence of the progressive and educated part of the people; but the non-progresive and turbulent elements have sought to use this religious movement for their own ends, while conjurers, dreamers, and other dangerous persons have multiplied stories and marvels, growing greater with each recital. Thus a distrust has grown up around the infected tribes, and a situation of difficulty and delicacy has come about."

3.   Greene, Jerome A. "The Sioux Land Commission of 1889 : Prelude to Wounded Knee." *South Dakota History*, 1(1):41-72(Winter 1970).

This is a highly detailed account of the Sioux Land Commission of 1889. From the initiation of the Fort Laramie Treaty in 1868, basically giving the land in South Dakota to the Sioux, through to the discovery of gold there in 1874, we read about the unsavory or outright dishonest attempts to regain the land in South Dakota.

Ultimately, the Sioux Land Commission was appointed, and Greene reviews first, the actual personnel of this committee, and then the actions taken, along with the related ramifications.

Admitting that direct military force was the immediate cause of the Wounded Knee Massacre, Greene blames the Land Commission for pressuring the Indians to give up their land, for pitting Indian against Indian, and for distracting the novice Indian farmers into letting their farms languish while they fought for the land itself. Almost nothing the Land Commission promised was fulfilled.

4.   Grinnell, George Bird. "Account of the Northern Cheyenne Concerning the Messiah Superstition." *Journal of American Folklore.* 4(12):61-69(1891).

This article concerning the Ghost Dance is especially interesting in that it is based on information gathered in November, 1890 from the Northern Cheyenne tribe at Fort Keogh in Wyoming. Grinnell's informants among the Cheyenne had been introduced to the notion of a messiah by the Arapaho and this group referred to the dance as the "Dance of Christ." Grinnell attended several dances of the Southern Cheyennes and the Southern Arapho.

Grinnell traces the origin of the Messiah Movement to Nevada, through a pilgimage made by an Arapaho named Sitting Bull, to attend the Ghost Dances there. Grinnell was able to attend several Ghost Dances himself, and his reports of his experiences of what was to become a major phenomenon for Native Americans is well focused and informative.

5.   Lee, Robert. "Messiah Craze Wounded Knee." *Wi-Iy-Iyohi,* Bulletin of the South Dakota Historical Society. 9(2) May 1, 1955.

This work contains a basic description of the initial Ghost Dance concept of Tavibo in Nevada, in 1870, a description of Wovoka's early life, and of his dreams during the eclipse of January 1, 1889. Wovoka begins spreading his message: "Work hard, don't fight with the whites, don't lie or steal, and dance the Ghost Dance, and the happy life of the past will return." This message spread very quickly to the Northeast, to the Dakota Sioux.

The article then outlines the Treaty of 1889, in which "all the lands in the Great Sioux Reservation outside of the separate reservations herein described, are hereby restored to the public domain." This land, approximately 11 million acres in what is now South Dakota, is here described in terms of its dollar value per acre. This treaty was to have been valid only with the signatures of 2/3 of the adult males, but this validity is in question. For example, neither Red Cloud nor Sitting Bull signed this treaty.

The rumor of the Messiah Movement made its way into the South Dakota region at this time, and here we read about the Sioux delegation to Nevada to investigate this possibility of salvation, and about the arrest of some of this group upon their return to the Dakotas. The part of this group which did not get arrested was, coincidentally, responsible for interpreting Wovoka's basic message of peace into one of hostility and violence. Here the article reviews the input of Kicking Bear and Short Bull, members of the delegation responsible for this re-interpretation. Ghost Dance shirts -- supposedly bullet-proof against white men's bullets -- were also introduced at this time by these men.

Lee reviews the military build-up in the area and the changes in Agency personnel. Quotes from local newspapers reveal the concerns of the settlers. These, along with a detailed list of military garrisons and their commanders, supply the complete scenario for the Wounded Knee Massacre. An excellent map is included.

6.   Lowie, Robert H. *Indians of the Plains*.   Garden City, New York : [Published for the American Museum of Natural History].The Natural History Press, 1963, c.1954.

Lowie discusses the Ghost Dance as one of two modern religious movements among Native Americans -- the Ghost Dance and the Peyote Cult. He observes a brief history of the Ghost Dance, directly linking the 1870 movement and its leader to a relative of Wovoka, the leader of the movement of 1889-1890. The issue of Wovoka's involvement with Christianity plays an important part in this discussion, with the prophet probably pretending to be the messiah himself.

The greater success of the movement in 1890 is suggested to have been attributable to two reasons: 1) greater access to travel and communication, and 2) by 1888, the Indians in the Northwest were destitute: the buffalo had all but disappeared, misunderstandings with the U.S. government had proliferated, and the Teton Dakota, the Cheyenne, the Arapaho, and the Kiowa siezed upon what they considered to be their new faith, though they actually changed its original import completely.

7.   McGregor, James H., Superintendant U.S.I.S., Retired. *The Wounded Knee Massacre from the Viewpoint of the Sioux*. Baltimore : Wirth Brothers, 1940.

The superior character of the Sioux is described in intimate detail by this retired Indian agent, and specifically contrasted with the questionable treatment of the Indians by various government bodies and officers.

The movements of the band of Sioux led by Big Foot after Sitting Bull's death, prior to the Wounded Knee Massacre are traced. The actual battle is detailed through a series of statements: first from participating U.S. military officials and other white observers, and then, through the statements of 25 Sioux survivors of the massacre.

8.   McKern, Sharon S. and Thomas McKern. "The Peace Messiah" *Mankind* 2(97):58-69(1970).

Written with the prose style of a screenplay, this article draws a vivid portrait of the Indian world at the end of the 19th century, a time of desolation and despair for the Indian. It was also the time of the growth of the Ghost Dance. The McKerns trace the spread of this Movement initiated by Wovoka in Nevada, alternating the presentation of the facts with a kind of universal, all-knowing narration. They trace his life from his boyhood, through the height of the Ghost Dance Movement and finally to his death "in obscurity in 1932...."(sic)

This article is somewhat puzzling. It offers some apparently little-known facts regarding Wovoka's life. His stay in the Puget Sound area, and his contact with the Shaker cults there, for example, along with his participation in "more than a few of the frenzied trance ceremonies" of that cult could explain the source of some parts of what was to become the Ghost Dance ceremony.

Although the article is full of third person stream-of-consciousness re-telling of the experience of the Ghost Dance, and their sympathy with the stricken Indians involved is heartwarming, the report of the death of Sitting Bull is questionable. It is combined with the actual Wounded Knee Massacre, such that "the revered old Chief submitted peaceably when arrested in his cabin but once he was taken outside, shots were fired and within five minutes, more than two hundred Indians lay dead or dying...." The McKerns lose a certain amount of credibility here. There are several excellent photographs.

9.   "Masking The Frauds." *Illustrated American.* 5:544(February 7, 1891).

The public excitement and dismay regarding the "distressed condition of the poor Sioux" are implied in this article. The problems encountered in posting a petition requesting inquiries into the Wounded Knee incident, the behaviour of the military, the actions of General Nelson A. Miles and the actions of the Seventh Cavalry are also recounted. The article was published one month and six days after the Wounded Knee Massacre. *The Illustrated American* was a popular magazine in which this article was a feature. The editors were nevertheless very serious regarding these problems. The article not only names "Commissioner Morgan, who controled the Indian Bureau," who was apparently named in the petition, as well as Secretary Nobel; it also quotes Professor Otis T. Mason, curator of the Department of Ethnology, saying, "I think the military are to blame for all this trouble, and that the presidential aspirations of General Miles and the desire of the Seventh Cavalry to revenge Custer's death precipitated the fight at Wounded Knee."

10.   Maus, Marion, Lieutenant, U.S.Army. "The New Indian Messiah" *Harper's Weekly*, June 6, 1890.

This article was published in the summer of 1890 when the Ghost Dance Movement had gained a sizable profile in South Dakota. Maus and his friend, Frederick Remington were accompanying General Nelson A. Miles and the Northern Cheyenne Commission. Maus and Remington visited the scene of a Ghost Dance at the Pine Ridge Agency. There they had the opportunity to talk to several apostles of this new religion. They talked to Red Cloud, Porcupine, Sitting Bull, and Little Wound, among others. The individual statements of these apostles make up the substance of this article.

The experiences of these apostles were all somewhat different, but the message of the Ghost Dance Movement was strong enough to elicit an article like this one in this national magazine. This article does not refer at all to the massive military presence which accompanied General Miles. The last paragraph does, however, refer vaguely to a possible Mormon influence on the initial Ghost Dance prophecy.

11.   Meighan, Clement W. and Riddell, Francis A. *The Maru Cult of the Pomo Indians : A California Ghost Dance Survival*. Highland Park, Los Angeles : Southwest Museum, 1972. [Southwest Museum Papers (no. 23)]

This monograph discusses the present day Maru religion of the Pomo Indians as a direct descendant of the famous California Ghost Dance of 1870. Viewed as a revivalistic movement, the participants would necessarily revert to their old ways. The plains Indians revived their old warrior ways, leading to the conflict with the U.S. military. In California, however, the Indians revived their old public ceremonies, built large dance houses, and strengthened their patterns of ceremonial life in a way still remembered today.

As the authors state in the introduction, their aim in this monograph is to increase the understanding of revivalistic cults in general, through a painstaking historical analysis of one particular cult.

This book contains much illustration: drawings of the various kinds of *houses* or buildings used for the ceremonies; costumes and religious regalia; dance formation and diagrams of the different dance steps.

12.   Miller, David Humphreys. *Ghost Dance.*   Lincoln and London :
       University of Nebraska, 1985, 1959.

       Unimpressed by accounts of the Ghost Dance written by white
       contemporaries of the Ghost Dance which are "obviously slanted for the
       unknowing or bigoted white readers of their time," Miller has "gotten
       this story direct from Indians who were themselves Ghost Dancers, or
       were otherwise involved in the religious excitement." He has taken the
       accounts of one hundred and thirty-five men and women from 25
       different tribes.

       Miller began his research in 1935. Through extended close contact with
       these informants, a tightly woven history is constructed: the history of
       the Sioux Ghost Dance war, 1890-1891.

       He begins with an outline of the reservations in South Dakota --
       Cheyenne River, Standing Rock, Pine Ridge, Rosebud; Toungue River in
       Montana; Wind River in Wyoming; Kiowa in Oklahoma and Walker
       River in Nevada. He lists the Agents responsible for these reservations,
       followed by a list of the Indian leaders associated with each reservation.
       This is followed by names of whites involved at each agency. He then
       lists his most valuable contacts -- personal friends -- among the Indians,
       which include Black Elk, Iron Hand, Frank Kicking Bear (son of Kicking
       Bear), Chief Ben American Horse.

13.   Mooney, James. *The Ghost Dance Religion and the Sioux Outbreak of
       1890.* Chicago and London : Phoenix Books, 1896, 1965.

       James Mooney compiled this material regarding the 1890-1891 Ghost
       Dance Movement in the years 1891, 1892 and 1893. In these years,
       following the Wounded Knee Massacre, Mooney traveled a total of
       32,000 miles, visiting twenty separate Indian tribes in his investigation
       of the Ghost Dance.

       He began his study of the Ghost Dance in Oklahoma, with the Arapaho,
       Cheyenne, Kiowa, Commanche, Apache, Caddo, and the Wichita. These
       inquiries subsequently led him to Wovoka, the prophet of the Ghost
       Dance. Traveling to Nevada, he was able to secure an interview with
       him, to talk with him about the Ghost Dance. This meeting is detailed,
       and forms the basis of much of the rest of Mooney's work here. The
       doctrine of the Ghost Dance is examined through reviewing the
       conversation with Wovoka and through a letter written by an Arapaho

who attended a meeting between Wovoka and a group from his tribe. This letter explains this new religion, and elaborates on the social requirements of the belief. Additional documents from other sources include a pamphlet, anonymously published from a Mormon group in Salt Lake City; an acccount from Porcupine, the Arapaho who had traveled to meet the Ghost Dance messiah; a record of an interview regarding the Ghost Dance with Kwapi, a Yankton; and one from George Sword, an Oglala. These and the many other records included with them, describe the basis of the Ghost Dance as it was understood in the various areas from which they came. They also reveal the attitudes of the participants and other interested parties.

Mooney investigates the spread of the religion in California, tracing its movement there to the Pacific Ocean in the west, south to Potrero, and north to the Pit River group.

The participation of the Sioux, east of the Rockies is also traced. The cut in the government rations to them is detailed and documented. Mooney describes the growth of the belief in South Dakota after the six person delegation of inquiry sent to Nevada returned. Short Bull and Kicking Bear were among these delegates returning to spread the word of the messiah. The specific military personnel are described and statements from several of these are provided. Troop movements and allocations are outlined. The account of the outbreak is accomplished with vivid detail.

Mooney's participation in the Ghost Dance on several occasions and in various locations enabled him to understand the ceremonies and especially the music. He interprets the ceremonies, the sacred objects used, even the trances. He also includes a great number of the songs used, the texts as well as the musical notation.

This work is especially valuable in its objectivity. As a result of Mooney's concern for this subject and his willingness to explore all available avenues into the matter, he has discovered and included the wealth of information presented here. Some of these materials contained in this document are contradictory. Many of the questions raised have no precise answers. Nevertheless, the data presented in this book has provided the primary core of information on this subject, as well as a model of investigation for anthroplogists, ethnographers and historians.

14.   Moorehead, W.K. "Ghost Dancing in the West : Origin and Development of the Messiah Craze and the Ghost Dance." [New York] : *Illustrated American*.4(48):327-333(January 17, 1891).

Moorehead was a reporter assigned to the Pine Ridge Agency in 1889-1890. He was witness to the rise of the Messiah Craze. He saw the attempts first of Agent H.G. Gallagher, and then Agent D.F. Royer of Pine Ridge, to control and then to curtail the celebration of the Ghost Dance. Moorehead himself attended Ghost Dance celebrations and here describes these events in detail. His report is fairly objective, sympathizing with the Sioux, their desparate condition and the unconscionable way they were treated by the U.S. Federal government. His description of the dance includes the clothes worn, the sweat-houses, and music, complete with scores as well as English translations of the words. Lithographs of some of the scenes around Pine Ridge and of the dances are also included.

15.   Pfaller, Father Louis. "The Indian Scare of 1890." *North Dakota History* 39(2):7-17(1972). Bismark : State Historical Society of North Dakota.

Father Pfaller gives an account of the tension which grew in North Dakota as a result of the Ghost Dance Movement.

The Sioux, the Cheyenne, the Arikara tribes were, on the one hand, only recently confined to reservation life, and on the other hand, just in the process of learning about the Ghost Dance. Even though the Indians living on most of the numerous agencies in the area were, by and large, peaceful by 1890, for those tribes mentioned, dissatisfaction and discontent prevailed and enthusiasm for the Ghost Dance grew. With the Indian policy of reservation living, the military had been in the process of reducing its forces since 1876, after the Custer Battle. However, as the North Dakota spring passed into summer and fall in 1890, this decision seemed, to the settlers, ill-advised.

As the Ghost Dance Movement grew and became more threatening to the whites, the military presence was again restructured in the area. There were numerous letters of alarm sent to the Indian Agents and to the Commissioner of Indian Affairs.

Father Pfaller gives a good account of the fear that swept over North Dakota, with specific incidents which involved towns thrown into panic as a result of the Indian enthusiasm over the Ghost Dance.

16.   Phister, Nat. P. First Lt., U.S.A.,"The Indian Messiah." *The American Anthropoligist*, 4(2):105-108(1891).

This brief article, on the Ghost Dance and the Messiah, was published in April of 1891, four months after the Wounded Knee Massacre. It was probably written to <u>inform</u> an already nervous public. Phister mentions "a great many articles having been written...more or less correct, but none entirely satisfactory." He apparently had been in Nevada and had been able to personally investigate the matter and, after "talking to many in Nevada on the subject," felt himself "able to give a very correct account of the tenets of the faith."

The account actually covers an array of information concerning the Ghost Dance in 1869 and the one started by a prophet's son in 1889, whom Phister calls *Kvit-tsow*. His information is <u>mostly</u> consistent with other published information concerning the Ghost Dance out of Nevada. His information, however, includes a fulfillment date of May 1892. He also refers to an elusive character named Johnson Sides, as a "claimant to the Messiahship of his people" but who is really "sensible and knows *Kvis-tsow* is crazy and that his doctrine is pernicious."

17.   Stewart, Omer C. "The Ghost Dance," in *Anthropology on the Great Plains,* edited by W. Raymond Wood and Margot Liberty, 178-187. Lincoln and London : University of Nebraska Press, 1980.

This is a critical discussion of James Mooney and his book, *The Ghost Dance Religion and the Sioux Outbreak of 1890,*[1896] and of other documents written by parties directly involved with that event, i.e., letters written by General Nelson A. Miles, commander of the U.S. military in South Dakota during the 1989-90 Ghost Dance troubles and J.T. Morgan's Report of the Commissioner for Indian Affairs. Also discussed are works by other ethnologists who have studied this affair.

Stewart disagrees with Mooney regarding the basic cause of the outbreak. He cites many other ethnographers and historians, as well as military participants involved at the Pine Ridge Reservation with the event and concludes: "...the Ghost Dance among the Sioux had little or nothing to do wiith the 'Sioux outbreak' of 1890... ." Stewart lays the responsibility, instead, on General Nelson A. Miles, commander of the military at the Pine Ridge Reservation at the time of the outbreak, and on his mistaken belief that the Ghost Dance was a cover for a dangerous conspiracy. The essay is also directly critical of Mooney and of the influence that his reports and discussion had on the military action taken.

18.   Tibbles, Thomas Henry. *Buckskin and Blanket Days : Memoirs of a Friend of the Indians*. Lincoln : University of Nebraska Press, 1957.

In the last half of his life, Thomas H. Tibbles was a newspaper correspondent, along with his second wife. Both were assigned to cover the unfolding story at the Pine Ridge Agency in South Dakota as tension mounted there.

This romantic autobiographical work reveals Tibbles' life in the 'old west,' where he was frequently in the company of Indians and made close friends. After working as a free lance reporter during the Civil War, he became a circuit preacher in 1871. In 1879 he pledged himself to the cause of the Ponca Tribe with their problems of relocation, and participated in the historic court case which resulted in the judge's decision that "an Indian is a person." He married the daughter of an Omaha Indian Chief and, in 1883 they homesteaded in Nebraska. However, in 1888, they leased the farm, and by 1890, both were working as reporters, assigned to the Pine Ridge Agency to cover the news happening there.

Several chapters of this book deal with the incident at Wounded Knee and the Ghost Dance, amidst the overflow of newspaper correspondents. Tibbles and his wife stayed with friends acquired years in the past, an Indian family, "where we could hear facts instead of fiction." His understanding of the Indians in the area reflects a group of people who had gathered at the Agency with the hope of getting rations which had been severely cut. Tibbles relates the sequence of events: the Dawes Act had been passed, but not yet applied in South Dakota; and the government officials had decided to cut the rations to the tribe in an effort to force the Indians into farming, land for which was not yet allotted and for which the tribe had no equipment. The people Tibbles and his wife were with had no major affection for the sudden craze for ghost dancing in ghost shirts. They said, "Four of our friends had actually made a long journey up into the mountains to see and talk with the messiah, and he had given them instructions about the dance." And, "Its a peace dance. No one is allowed even to carry a weapon of war nearer than half a mile to the place where the dance is held."

The situation at the Pine Ridge Agency got worse. Tibbles' friends became more and more anxious about the increasing number of military forces accumulating in the area. While Tibbles and his wife continued reporting the situation to be tense but peaceful, the other reporters, for more interesting news, were exaggerating the situation into one of war and dire straights. The townspeople were experiencing a new flow of business resulting from the great number of military forces who needed their services. The Tibbles' lives were in danger from the hostility to their straightforeward reporting.

The Massacre at Wounded Knee is vividly described. Tibbles had ridden horseback out to the area where the Indian council was meeting with the army. He had started back and was a half hour away when he heard gun shots. His narrative of the events which followed is graphic.

19.   Watson, Elmo Scott. "The Last Indian War, 1890-91 - A Study of Newspaper Jingoism." *Journalism Quarterly*. 20:205-219(1943).

Watson details here the "Exploitation of the 'last of the Indian wars...'", by newspaper correspondents anxious to get something in the newspapers in the larger centers of population -- either New York, Chicago, Denver, or on the west coast. He mentions the fact that the "hostilities at Wounded Knee" drew more correspondents than ever before -- at least 25 -- for any military event. These correspondents are individually identified, along with the newspapers for which they worked. The general practice of "exaggeration, distortion and plain faking" had already begun 25 years before during the Red Cloud War of 1866-1867 with "sensational and almost uniformly inaccurate newspaper accounts of its events...." Watson compares newspaper reports published in South Dakota and Nebraska to those communicated from there to newspapers based in the east, finding the local reports much more realistic and truthful.

Contemporary accusations of "alarmist work" were gererally directed at "space writers" and these accusations usually assumed the basic reason for these inaccuracies to be the money to be gained by the reporter. Watson points out, however, another probable reason: these reporters were "serving local interest when [they] wrote propaganda, disguised as news, to influence the federal government into sending more troops to the 'threatened' areas, thereby adding to the profits of tradesmen in the frontier towns." Another possible reason for these "exaggerations" in the press, could have been that, having spent time in the frontier, among the settlers, with the threat of hostile Indians ever-present, these reporters often had, like the settlers, the cliched opinion, of "the only good Indian is a dead one." They <u>were</u> reflecting the sentiments of many of the local inhabitants.

Watson traces the course of the months preceeding the Wounded Knee Massacre in terms of the increasing number of inflamatory reports submitted to the newspapers in Washington, D.C., New York, etc., with their impressions of increasing peril in the South Dakota area, the responsible military personnel responding with increased military presence, and the Indians responding to this presence by attempting to withdraw to the Dakota Bad Lands. This response is read and reported by the reporters as yet another act of hostility. The "timorous and inept agent at Pine Ridge," Dr. D.F. Royer is characterized as one who "lacked nearly all of the qualities necessary for handling successfully the potentially explosive situation at Pine Ridge at that time." Royer's inability to control the real troubles plaguing the Pine Ridge agency led him to play right into the hands of these propagandists and request more armed forces to come to his assistance. The relevant personnel involved, on both sides of this unfortunate and confused activity, are chronologically linked to their respective roles. Included are "the high priests of the Ghost Dance," Short Bull and Kicking Bear, a group of Ogalalas and several bands of Brule Sioux from the Rosebud Reservation, Two Strike, Crow Dog, Big Foot and his band of Miniconjous, President Harrison, Gen. John R. Brooke, Maj. S.M. Whitside, Col. J.W. Forsyth and Gen. Nelson A. Miles.

These are the major players in this incident, which gained nearly all of its momentum from reports conceived with several possible intentions and usually with some purpose in mind. But objective, informative reporting of the news from South Dakota was rare. However, Watson, "a recognized authority on the newspaper coverage of Indian uprisings," ends his article with this acknowledgment: "...newspaper correspondents who covered conflicts with the Indians -- even this 'phony war' of 1890-91 -- did take far more risks than those journalists who have accompanied the armies in so-called 'civilized warfare.'"

20.   Zanjani, Sally S. "The Indian Massacre That Never Happened." *Nevada Historical Society Quarterly.* 20(2):119-129(1988).

This paper addresses the question "Why did Nevada escape the carnage that happened in Wounded Knee?" Some of the newspapers in Nevada were actively inciting the whites with dramatically exaggerted and even false descriptions of the Ghost Dances, participation in which had, by that time achieved full momentum, and with highly exagerated or wholly false population statistics of the Indians. However, Acting Governor Frank Bell had taken office until January, 1891. He was replaced by Roswell K. Colcord in January, 1891. Both were mature men in their '50's and were committed to a policy of restraint. Colcord refused to reinforce military posts in the area. He also refused to break up the Ghost Dances. Together, they were assisted by the state's top military official, Acting Adjutant General C.H. Galousha, who shared their attitude of "calm and restraint."

These men as well as a few others, are cited by Zanjani as responsible for the relative peace in Nevada during the Ghost Dance Movement there in 1889 and 1890. Newspaper articles and correspondence hotly criticizing their decisions are related and the situation in the Dakotas is compared to these events in Nevada.

2
Tribal Histories

21.   Andrist, Ralph K. *The Long Death : the Last Days of the Plains Indians.*
New York, London : Collier & Macmilian, 1964, 1970.

Andrist presents a fully documented history reviewing the demise of the
tribes of Plains Indians, from the Great Lakes to the west coast. From
the uprising of the Minnisota Santee Sioux in 1862 through the
massacre of the Indians at Wounded Knee in 1890, Andrist recounts the
specific steps taken in the crushing of the Sioux, the Cheyenne, the Nez
Perce, the Modocs, the Bannocks and the Utes -- virtually all the tribes
of Plains Indians. He details the political, economic and social designs
of the government and the private individuals involved. Included are 22
pages of photographs and 21 maps.

Vivid portraits of the leaders on both sides are drawn, including Red
Cloud, Black Kettle, Crazy Horse, Sitting Bull and Chief Joseph. U.S.
army personnel Generals Sheridan, Custer and Miles as well as other
non-Indian individuals are quoted and their involvment outlined.

The Ghost Dance Movement in the Dakotas is examined as a last
desperate hope of salvation in the ebbing life of the Plains Indians. The
massacre at Wounded Knee is depicted as the culmination of the Anglo-
Indian relationship in the 19th century.

22.   Debo, Angie. *A History of the Indians of the United States.* Norman : University of Oklahoma Press, 1970, 1983.

This is a general history of Indian - white relations in the United States: the on-going, intrinsic insensitivity of the Federal government to the culture of the Indians, as the whites began, almost immediately upon civil interaction, to acculturate the Indian into white ways. The specific losses for the Indian are discussed here.

The Ghost Dance Movement, in 1890 in South Dakota is traced, through Wovoka, spreading to the Shoshoni, the Bannock, the Crow, the Cheyenne and Arapaho. However, when spring came and the "expected deliverance" was not forthcoming, the Movement among these tribes, collapsed.

The Sioux, however, were entering their toughest season -- winter -- without rations, food, supplies of any kind, and by 1889, their land was reduced to an almost unrecognizably small size. Emotionally, they invested heavily in the Ghost Dance. The tragedy of Sitting Bull's death was only the beginning of the end. The telling of these events is well documented, with military documents, newspaper articles and with reference to noted historians.

23.   Forbes, Jack D. *Nevada Indians Speak : Selections Edited with Introduction and Commentary.* Reno : University of Nevada Press, 1967.

This is an anthology of Indian grass roots insights into the history of the western United States in general, and specifically, into the history of the Great Basin and white-Indian contact. The Northern Paiutes and the Western Shoshonis have, through the years, been more vocal, and so they are here also, having left a recorded documentation of themselves. The collection includes some documents posibly derogatory towards Indians. The language, spelling, punctuation, etc., from the original sources, have been preserved.

Listed under "Adventist - Ghost Dance doctrine," discussion regarding Ghost Dance Movements occurs several times, sequentially, in the chronology presented. These are observations by local individuals, personally involved.

A lengthy quote from James Mooney is included. Also included is an item from Wovoka requesting a land allotment in 1912.

24.   Hyde, George E. *A Sioux Chronicle*. Norman : University of Oklahoma, 1956.

This is Hyde's second book on the history of the Sioux. The first, *Red Cloud's Folk* (Norman, 1937) is the history of the tribe up to the end of The Sioux Wars, 1876-77. This second book deals with the Sioux as a captive people on the reservation in Dakota trying to deal with the several U.S. government agencies which had controlling, sometimes contratictory or conflicting authority over them, instituting various plans and Indian policies.

The period between 1878 and 1891, from the standpoint of the Sioux, is described. The attempts to force the tribe into farming, into white schools, and the tribe's relative success at cattle ranching are some of the factors we read about.

The Ghost Dance Movement is the focus of the last quarter of the book. The involvement is traced from the introduction of the notion of an Indian messiah, first received by mail at the Pine Ridge Agency and investigated in Nevada by a select group of Sioux leaders: Good Thunder, Cloud Horse, Yellow Knife, Short Bull, Flat Iron, Broken Arm, Kicking Bear and Sitting Bull (Oglala).

The Ghost Dance Movement spread through the Sioux Nation very quickly and was, by and large, recieved and embraced. Details of the reception given the Movement at the several Indian agencies by the Indians and their attendant Agents, e.g. Dr. D.R. Royer and James McLaughlin, are given. The Indian's desperate attempt to attain life as they had known it in their past is outlined step by step in the specific history of the Ghost Dance in and around the Agencies of the Dakotas in 1889-1891. Hyde describes the Ghost Dance participation of Red Cloud, Sitting Bull, Crazy Horse, Little Wound and others. There is also a detailed account of Sitting Bull's death.

This book is more detailed than most in tracing the events leading up to the desparate situation resulting in the Wounded Knee Massacre.

25.   Johnson, Edward C. *Walker River Paiutes : A Tribal History*. Schurz, Nevada : Walker River Paiute Tribe, 1975.

Edward Johnson, a tribal member of the Walker River Paiute tribe, was assisted in this monograph by the tribal Chairman, Melvin D. Thom, and another tribe member, Stannard Frank, who was the interviewer. The research brought to bear in this compilation of the history of this Nevada tribe includes the National Archives, BIA records, U.S. military records, state records of Nevada, California, and historical records of the Church of Jesus Christ of Latter-Day-Saints [Mormons].

The record begins with a short review of the probable life of the tribe in the pre-European-contact period, and moves into recorded history from 1820 through the formation of reservations for the Nevada Indians. Included is a review of "The Ghost Dance Prophets (1860-1895)."

The discussion of this phase of the life of the tribe includes the history of Wodziwob, their shaman of the late 1860's and 1870 who prophesied the dead would return if the people would do the dance he called the Ghost Dance. The Paiute response to his teachings, as well as that of the local whites, the Indian Agents and the military is discussed. Wodziwob, also called Fish Lake Joe (possibly because he was from the region of Fish Lake) was a practicing native doctor until his death in 1918. One of his followers was Tavibo, father of Wovoka. The life of Wovoka is traced and the details of the 1889-1890 Ghost Dance Movement are given. Included are quotes from local newspapers, as well as correspondence of local Indian Agents, local whites, and the military, on the subject of both of the Ghost Dance Movements.

The book continues to outline the history of the tribe, into the 20th century, and includes a list of Walker River Tribal Leaders from 1850 through 1974, as well as the "Chronology of Events Affecting the Walker River People (1776-1974)."

26.   Knack, Martha C. and Omer C. Stewart. *As Long as the River Shall Run : An Ethnohistory of Pyramid Lake Indian Reservation*. Berkeley/Los Angeles/London : University of California, 1984.

This is an ethnohistorical examination of the Pyramid Lake Indian Reservation, over a 120 year period, as their resources were expropriated, their waters cut off, and they were crowded into a smaller and smaller space. The book carefully examines the changes in the lives of the natives of this area, in the physical characteristics of the land, and in the economic structure of the populations involved. These changes were generated by prolonged contact with the whites and their legal and illegal pressures.

The discussion of the Ghost Dances, both the 1870 and the 1890 movements, is approached, first by describing the tradition of the shaman learning the dance in the spirit world and passing it along to the populace, and then, by documenting the denigration of this tradition by the local whites, who basically failed to take either of these movements seriously. It was noted, however, by an inspector at Walker Lake [in 1870] that all the members of the Paiute tribe there were participating in the Ghost Dance.

27.   Lesser, Alexander. *The Pawnee Ghost Dance Hand Game : Ghost Dance Revival and Ethnic Identity*. Madison : University of Wisconsin Press, 1978.

Lesser wrote this book initially in 1932. It is devoted primarily to traditional Pawnee religion and philosophy. In the course of his investigations, he discovered the "tremendous impact" the Ghost Dance doctrines of the 1890's had had on the Pawnee people and the "creative emergence in those years of the Pawnee Ghost Dance Hand Games."

The Pawnee response to the Ghost Dance was more than one of religious excitement. For the Pawnee, it was a reviving of their old customs and ceremonies. It served as an encouragement to the old religious leaders and groups of leaders to remember the rites and traditional customs which were, in 1890, all but forgotten. The remembered traditions, passed along from old generation to new, stayed with the Pawnee into the beginning of the 20th century.

By the 1930's, however, most of the meaningful traditional religious ceremonies were again gone, as were the traditional personnel to perform them. The Hand Games had lost their traditional religious meaning, but had become occasions for recreation and sport. And so they are now [1977]. Now they are part of the tribal tradition and identity retained by the Pawnees, along with their language and tribal history.

Lesser's book details the history and society of the Pawnee Tribe from the first white contact, into the Ghost Dance of 1889-1890, and into the twentieth century. His discussion of the actual spread of the Ghost

Dance Movement from Nevada and evenually to the southern plains is quite detailed. The Pawnee involvment with Wovoka and the Movement is described. The Ghost Dance Hand Game is described in depth, in its history and tribal significance.

28. Robinson, Doane. *A History of the Dakota Sioux Indians,* by Doane Robinson, Secretary of the South Dakota Department of History. Minneapolis : Ross & Haines, Inc., 1967.

This is an extremely detailed history of the Sioux Indians, from their earliest traditions and first contact with white men to the final settlement of the last of them on reservations and their subsequent abandonment of the old tribal life.

The machinations of the various branches of the government of the U.S. (Bureau of Indian Affairs, U.S. military, Presidential involvement, etc.), each vying for control over the Indians, and over the western land and its potential and its resources, spelled misery for the Indians. Robinson's book traces many specific "questionable" policies and actions, which resulted in the withholding of rations and supplies promised to the Indians in the winter of 1890. Many starved to death as a result. Also reviewed are the treaties and land agreements reached with the Indians, and how these agreements came about.

The last chapter discusses the Ghost Dance, beginning with the eclipse of January 1, 1889 when Wovoka recieved the instructions for the Ghost Dance. Robinson reviews the communications from the Paiutes to the Sioux of South Dakota. William Selwyn, in his capacity as postmaster at the Rosebud Agency in South Dakota in 1889, became aware of the Ghost Dance and its implications. Selwyn's letter to Agent Royer at the Pine Ridge Agency, describing the the growth and importance of this movement was, unfortunately officially ignored.

The North Dakota Sioux, however, sent emissaries to Nevada to investigate. These included Short Bull, Kicking Bear, Red Cloud and Man Afraid of His Horses.

This book is a solid historical review of Sioux tribal history, as nearly as can be traced, and addresses the Ghost Dance from the perspective of its being one of the unfortunate experiences resulting from European contact.

29.   Ruby, Robert H . *The Oglala Sioux : Warriors in Transition.* New York: Vantage Press, Inc. 1955.

This brief review of the Oglala Sioux is compiled from letters Ruby has recieved from his Indian acquaintances. Included are two biographical sketches of Red Cloud and Crazy Horse -- which do not refer to the Ghost Dance Movement.

The chapter "The Battle of Wounded Knee" offers a brief description of the Ghost Dance Movement and traces the weeks and days and finally the hours leading up to the Massacre itself. He also provides several possible scenarios of an Indian initiation of the Massacre. One account is related by Dewey Beard, an Indian and veteran of both the Custer battle and the Battle At Wounded Knee. The account of the South Dakota Historical Society is also provided.

Finally, Ruby reviews the overall treatment the Indians have recieved from the federal government, then and up to the time this book was written (1955).

30.   Schusky, Ernest L. *The Forgotten Sioux : An Ethnohistory of the Lower Brule Reservation.* Chicago : Nelson-Hall, 1975,

This conscientious tribal history of the Lower Brule Sioux, is traced from before white civilization came and populated their land, through the 19th and 20th centuries, up to the 1970's when this book was published.

The main theme here is the on-going relationship of the Indians to the white government which took control of the Indian population, and the inconsistencies inherent in the policies adopted, as well as the hardships these misguided policies caused.

The discussion of the response to these hardships in the form of the Ghost Dance in 1890 is pursued through letters between U.S. federal officials, local newspaper articles, contemporary eye-witnesses and participants, contemporary and subsequent observers and historians.

The research through local primary sources and careful examination of the records and the correspondence of the Bureau of Indian Affairs provides a clear focus on the progress of life on the Lower Brule Indian Reservation through the 19th and 20th century

31.   Utley, Robert M. *The Last Days of the Sioux Nation.* New Haven and
       London : Yale University Press, 1963.

       This comprehensive work chronicles the last decade of the Sioux Indians
       in North and South Dakota, with documentation of specific Indian
       leaders, U.S. military reports and eye-witness accounts.

       This is a history of the Sioux Nation, the tribe for whom the Ghost
       Dance was most portentous. The history is well documented by United
       States government documents, military journals and periodicals,
       contemporary newspapers, material from the National Archives written
       by military figures participating in military events, letters and
       interviews with participants.

       Utley especially details the agreements between the U.S. government,
       military leaders and the Indians in tracing the demise of the Sioux
       Nation. Some of the leading figures he includes are Brig. Gen. John R.
       Brooks, Capt. Allyn Capron, Maj. Gen. George Crook, Col. James W.
       Forsyth, Maj. Gen. Nelson A. Miles, Kicking Bear, Red Cloud, Short
       Bull, Sitting Bull and Wovoka.

       Twenty photographs of some of the persons involved are also included.

32.   Utley, Robert M. *The Indian Frontier of the American West, 1846-1890.*
       Albuquerque : University of New Mexico Press, 1984.

       Robert Utley has teamed up with Ray Billington and hundreds of other
       scholars to produce this outstanding book of the American Western
       Frontier and its inhabitants, their lives and their relationships. In the
       process of discussing dozens of individual tribes, several specific
       observations occur: the institution of reservation living may have been
       the worst enemy the Indian faced, not the white man or his Hotchkiss
       guns. Another may have been the well-intentioned but unaware
       reformer who was able to hold such sway over the federal government
       policies regarding Indians.

33.   Vestal, Stanley. *New Sources of Indian History, 1850-1891 : The Ghost
       Dance and the Prairie Sioux : A Miscellanay.* Norman : University of
       Oklahoma Press, 1934.

This book is a collection of primary documents collected during a five year sojourn among the Sioux, researching the life and times of Sitting Bull. Here is presented a collection of personal letters, reports, even scraps of paper with connecting information written in pencil, for example, a note written to Sitting Bull from a female admirer and teacher, warning him not to become involved in the Ghost Dance Movement.

These letters and papers from officials, white citizens, Indians and close friends of Indians, is a very intimate view into the spirit of the times in South Dakota in the dacades between 1850 and 1890. In addition, there are included comments by Indians in the chapters titled "On warfare", "Notes on Individuals" [Indians] and the "Hunkpapa Sioux Calendar - 1801-1881."

This is a remarkable book, filled with juicy tidbits about and between people involved with, among other things, the Ghost Dance Movement.

3
Religion and the Ghost Dance

34.   Barney, Garold D. *Mormons, Indians and the Ghost Dance of 1890.*
        Lanham, Maryland : University Press of America, 1986.

        Research into the Mormon-Indian relationship, and the Mormon
        influence among the Plains Indians is documented by and large through
        the records of the Mormon church. This book examines the socio-
        religious conditions common to the Mormons in Utah and the Indians
        in the plains states in the last half of the 19th century.

        The religion inherent in the Ghost Dance is examined, and specifically
        the notion of a messiah is pursued as one major commonality, revivalism
        being another.

        This book deals mainly with the religious aspects of the Ghost Dance
        and examines the Anglo-Missionary influence on Wodziwob, Wovoka,
        Black Elk, Black Kettle and others.

35.   Coates, Lawrence G. "The Mormons and the Ghost Dance" *Dialog: A
        Journal of Mormon Thought.* 18(4):89-111(1985).

This paper was prepared for presentation to the Mormon History Association in conjunction with the Western History Conference in 1976. Its overall intent is to cite the ethnographers, historians, even participants in the events of the late 19th century American northwest who in any way allude to Mormon involvement with the Ghost Dance Movement. Coates denies any Mormom involvement. Mormon Church records are cited, documenting around 500 official Indian converts between 1850 and 1890. He notes claims of Mormon blame for the Ghost Dance in the writings of Paul Bailey, James Mooney, Gen. Nelson Miles, and others. He also comments that the notions of the end of the world, life after death of family and friend as well as self, special clothing and other ideas inherent in the Ghost Dance Movement came to the Plains Indians from California, through the Shaker religion there. This information he credits to Cora DuBois (1939).

In his conclusion, Coates writes, "close examination of the evidence shows that the Mormons did not conspire with the Indians in promoting the Ghost Dance."

36.   La Barre, Weston. *The Ghost Dance : Origins of Religion.* New York, New York : Dell Publishing Co., 1972.

In this work, La Barre equates religion in general to a Ghost Dance, tracing this human subjective capacity which has existed from prehistoric times through life in ancient Greece, into the 18th and 19th centuries. The book addresses world religious history, but there is a specific chapter (# 7) on the Ghost Dance in North America in 1870 and 1890.

This chapter begins in an outline of what happened to the Indians in the northwest United States in the last half of the 19th century, paraphrasing a number of other historians and ethnogaphers. The first sentence, "The two Ghost Dance movements represent the final catastrophe of Indian culture in the United States" is followed by a footnote, which cites 20 references. The chapter continues to detail the events concerning North American Indians and their participation in the Ghost Dance in response to the Anglo-American destruction of their culture. La Barre then includes outlines of other cultural incidents among other groups located in other parts of the world which had a similar response to an outside race intruding into and destroying their lives. Two of these cases are in Mongolia and New Guinea.

La Barres's point is that the commonality of the spiritual nature of this response is to be expected as a human response to this kind of cultural destruction.

37.   Lanternari, Vittorio. *The Religions of the Oppressed : A Study of Modern Messianic Cults.* New York : Alfred A. Knopf, 1963.

Lanternari's book is an historical investigation into religions generated by the loss of social, religious and political identity and cultural satisfaction among groups of primitive peoples. His studies extend to Africa, Melanesia, Polynesia, Asia and the Indian reservations of North America. Lanternari feels obligated in these studies to justify, or to "explain [for each religious movement] its nature, its function, and its genesis as well as its internal and external dynamics due to, respectively, factors in the culture and to the impact from other cultures and external forces."

The section on prophetic movements in North America reviews the 1799 Good Message cult, founded by the Iroquois, Handsome Lake in the Great Lakes area. Another movement is presented in his discussion of Mooney's evidence of an "outstanding forerunner of the Ghost Dance", a movement founded by a nameless Delaware prophet. This movement is based on a complete "rejection of all white customs and usages, including firearms...." The cult held the seeds that, years later would surface in movements started by Kanakud, Smohalla, Tenskwatawa and Wovoka.

Another religion treated is the Dreamer Cult. Raised in a community of Nez Perce and Yakima Indians, Smohalla (meaning preacher) led his people in the Columbia River region in Washington state in their rejection of what they considered the abuse of "Mother Earth" for profit [farming], in saving the earth for the return of their dead ancestors. Through an accident in 1860, Smohalla dissappeared for some months, was presumed dead and came back to life. His frequent trances and the messages obtained in them resulted in his being referred to as the Dreamer. The major active features of this cult consisted of performing several specific dances, especially the Dream Dance, regarded as a cure for "every ill introduced by the white man."

The Ghost Dance of 1870 among the Paviotso in Nevada and California, and its prophet, Wodziwob is discussed. Wodziwob's initial trance in 1869, and his dream of a huge train with all the Indians' ancestors on it is the beginning of this cult which, two years later and spreading "in two different directions, [would reach] all the tribes in the Western United States." The predominant theme here involved a "major cataclysm" that was expected to shake the entire earth, swallow the whites, leaving their buildings, tools and other goods for use by the Indians, who would be left unharmed. An assistant to Wodziwob named Numataivo (Tavibo) was the father of Wovoka, later named Jack Wilson. Another interesting aspect of the 1870 Ghost Dance is the Mormon involvement. The Mormons told the Indians that "by being baptized and going to church the old would all become young, the young men would never be sick...." Many Mormons joined the Ghost Dance cult, and many others joined Smohalla's Dreamers. The followers of Joseph Smith [Mormons], in 1892 felt Wovoka was the messiah foretold by Smith in 1840. Lanternari draws a parrallel between Wodziwob's Ghost Dance and its relationship with the Mormons and the Jehovah's Witnesses and the messianic movements of Africa "which produced the Kitawala cult."

Lanternari continues to describe other off-shoots from the Ghost Dance Movement, including the Earth Lodge cult, the Warm House cult and the Bole Maru cult. An extensive bibliography is included.

38.   Powers, William K. *Oglala Religion*. Lincoln, London : University of Nebraska Press, 1975,1977.

This book is an investigation into the culture and especially the society of the Oglala Sioux tribe, which has managed to maintain its religious, social and cultural identity from the initial invasion of Europeans through the Ghost Dance Movement into the 20th century. Powers makes several interesting points regarding the Oglala relationship to the Ghost Dance. Initially, the Ghost Dance Movement was quite alien to Oglala religion and cultural momentum. The notion of "a massive influx of deceased human and animal spirits that would be transformed back into their corporeal states..." would have been against the reincarnative system of the traditional Oglala beliefs.

However, on hearing of the messiah in Nevada, they sent a group to investigate and report back. They adapted the Ghost Dance to their own modes of expression. As a result, their religious leaders, who had lost most of their status as a result of the establishment of the reservation system and U.S. government control, began to regain their positions as the religious council and advisors regarding day to day dilemmas of reservation living. These sacred persons gave their people new hope and continued to lead even after the Ghost Dance ended, provided they maintained their ritual authority. "The content of the Oglala social relations changed; but the form, the structure, the relations between leader and follower persisted." This is a good piece of anthropology, original and well documented.

39.   Smoak, Gregory. "Mormons and the Ghost Dance of 1890." *South Dakota History*. 16(3):269-294(1986).

This article reviews the many accusations against the Mormon religious group of being the "prime movers" behind the Ghost Dance of 1890. Smoak quotes extensively from General Nelson A. Miles, who would eventually be the military commander of the cavalry at Wounded Knee Creek, and Lt. S.C. Robertson of the 1st Cavalry, interviewer of Porcupine, the Cheyenne Indian who, traveling from Wyoming, investigated the initial rumor of the Ghost Dance in Nevada. On his return he spread the word. Robertson became curious at Porcupine's several references to "the whites often dancing in it themselves," considering the Indian was referring to his travels through Mormon country. E.R. Kellogg, Commander of Fort Washakie, Wyoming, is quoted regarding the Arapaho and Shoshone of the Wind River Reservation. He was not concerned, but believed that representatives of the "Indian Christ" had been among them. He also felt that this "Indian Christ" was one "Bannack Jim (sic), a Mormon and it is not unreasonable to suppose that his attempts to stir up strife have been instigated by the Mormons."

Smoak gives a brief description of the history of the Mormon religion, and demonstrates its defensive postion with respect to the rest of the country. From its inception in Fayette, New York, to being hounded out of one place then another, this religious group, rejected partly because of its belief that the Indians were one of the 'lost tribes' referred to in the Old Testament. Mormonism is also based, by and large, on the notion of a gathering of "the people of Israel for the millennium." Due to their affection for the Indians, their social practices (polygamy), and their poor relationship with the federal government, the Mormon were "the logical scapegoat for the Ghost Dance troubles."

Many instances are described in which one or more Mormons could have played a part (e.g. groups of Indians investigating the Ghost Dance rumor, were confronted with the 'messiah' on successive nights, who appeared alternately as young, old, blond, dark-headed, bearded, etc.). The white robes of the Mormon ceremony were supposed to protect its wearer, and this notion may have been at the root of the concept of the

Ghost Dance shirt, which did not protect its wearer from the bullets of the white man. Most of the accusations against the Mormons came from people who needed to blame someone for the Ghost Dance. Government officials did not want to consider the consuming poverty to which the Indians had been reduced. The several governing bodies responsible for the Indians, -- the war department, the Bureau of Indian Affairs, were already laying the blame on each other. The general feeling was that the Ghost Dance religion could not have been initiated by the "heathen savages".

Ultimately, Smoak states "While the Mormons showed a keen interest in the movement, the fact remains that the Ghost Dance of 1890 was truly a pan-Indian movement. Many whites would not accept the Ghost Dance as an Indian response to the destruction of traditional tribal cultures, and thus they had to believe that more 'civilized' peoples had inspired and spread the religion. The Mormons were the obvious choice."

40.   Walker, James R. *Lakota Belief and Ritual.* Edited by Raymond J. DeMallie and Elaine A. Jahner. Lincoln, London : University of Nebraska Press; published in cooperation with the Colorado Historical Society, 1980.

James Walker was assigned to the Pine Ridge Agency in 1896 as the Doctor there. He eventually worked his way into the social establishment of the Oglala there, and became friends with many of them. He studied the traditional ways of dealing with disease, as well as everything else. He learned from the holy men of the tribes he dealt with. He was sucessful in enlisting their help in combating tuburculosis. His studies regarding the religion of the people he was responsible for was based in his desire to serve them medically. In this work, he has compiled a fascinating list of 'documents' or individual statements on specific aspects of religion from the old men in his care. Their statements make up the major part of this book.

Several of these documents deal with the Ghost Dance religion, and how it either affected these tribespeople, or exactly how they used it. One of these is quoted from Short Bull on the issue of "Sending spirits to the spirit world." Two other documents quoting Short Bull are included. Walker's conscientious investigation into the lives and priorities of the Sioux in and around the Pine Ridge Agency is a valuable tool for research regarding the Sioux in the aftermath of the Ghost Dance.

4

Personal Narratives
and Biographies

41. Adams, Alexander B. *Sitting Bull : An Epic of the Plains.* New York :
     Capricorn Books, G.P. Putnam's Sons, 1973.

This is a relatively sympathetic biography of the famous Hunkpapa
Sioux and the objectivity is refreshing.

The last chapter (p.350-364) deals with the military build-up in South
Dakota from 1876 to 1891. It also contains a very carefully outlined
description of the questionable political devices contrived by various
official commissions to "legally" arrange for the transfer of what really
amounted to most of South Dakota from the Indians to the U.S.
government.

A quick review of the Ghost Dance Movement, its history along with a
description of the participating and non-participating people, regarding
the Movement, begins the final portion of the book. We read of the
reaction of the local whites, and that of Agent James McLaughlin, to the
Ghost Dance and to Sitting Bull's participation in it.

The biography traces Sitting Bull's life and the circumstances of his
death as an integral part of the history of the area as well as the
government policies and politics.

42.   Bailey, Paul. *Ghost Dance Messiah*. Tucson : Westernlore Press, 1970, 1986.

This biography of Wovoka, also called Jack Wilson is recounted in the form of historical fiction in the personal detail which this approach allows. From Wovoka's relationship to his father, Tavibo, and Tavibo's death and Wovoka's being adopted by David Wilson and his family, Baily continues the story of Wovoka, turned 'Jack Wilson,' and his life as a dreamer, possible messiah to his people, the Walker Reservation and eventually the whole of the Plains, Basin, and Northwest territories.

Bailey's historical fiction reveals a strongly developed sense of history and an impressive control of the facts. He tells of young Jack Wilson learning the white man's language and religion, and the ways of the whites in general. Wilson/Wovoka is portrayed filtering all he had learned through his sense of life and existence as a functioning Paiute Indian. The history of this exceptional man, as related by Baily, the historian/writer is convincing, and it provides a credible, in-depth picture of the origin of the Ghost Dance.

43.   Bailey, Paul. *Wovoka, the Indian Messiah*. Los Angeles : Westernlore Press, 1957.

This biography of Wovoka begins with the man as a boy living with the Wilson family, a family of white, church going people who adopted him. The method employed in this book is one of intimate storytelling, detailing Wovoka's point of view. Bailey relies heavily on the work and 'on-the-spot field studies' of James Mooney. He also pays homage to Edward A. Dryer, an intimate friend of Wovoka's who was Mooney's interpreter during his visits with the "Paiute Messiah." Edward Dryer Jr. was also of great help to Bailey in providing his father's experiences as they were dictated and recorded.

In Yearington, Nevada, near the location of Wovoka's original trance, his original call to heaven, at the time Bailey was researching this book (early 1950's) there were still many residents available who remembered Wovoka, and Bailey has used their knowledge in putting together this biography. He has also used the photographic file of the American Ethnological Museum, as well as that of J. E. Reynolds. Another major source of study on Wovoka for Bailey is that of Col. Tim McCoy. McCoy's lifelong interest in the 'Wovoka legend', his work and his personal visit with the messiah is a meaningful addition to Bailey's collection of primary documentation.

Bailey has put together a solid portrait with the use of these intimate primary sources.

44.   Brininstool, E.A. *Fighting Indian Warriors : True Tales of the Wild Frontiers.* New York : Bonanza Books, 1953.

This is, chapter for chapter, a review of specific incidents occurring in the last half of the 19th century in the American west, between Indians and U.S. miltary. Brininstool admits frankly in the introduction to his sympathy for the Indians, and comments on "civilization's shame" inherent in the treatment of the Indians at the hands of the "civilization" which overtook them.

Each chapter deals with a specific event in colorful narrative. The source materials include records of anecdotal conversations with, and letters from Brininstool's "friends"..."both living and dead who rendered valuable information in the construction of this book." Although the book takes the form of historical fiction, one is convinced of the feeling throughout that Brininstool was either present at these events or really did know someone who had been.

His chapter "The Sioux Ghost Dance Trouble at Pine Ridge Agency, South Dakota, 1890," like his other discussions, is very intimate, and his more personal contacts are revealed in his elaboration of the Wounded Knee Massacre.

45.   Dangberg, Grace M. "Letters to Jack Wilson, the Paiute Prophet, Written Between 1908 and 1911." Smithsonian Institution Bureau of American Ethnology, Bulletin 164; Anthropological Papers, 55:279-296.

This collection of letters was preserved by Carrie Wilson, wife of J.I. Wilson, one of the boys in the family which adopted Jack Wilson (Wovoka) as a child. Carrie and her son, Joseph, had been responsible for reading them to Jack, and for answering them, initially. They are, by and large, letters requesting domestic advice, ceremonial equipment or Ghost Dance paraphernalia, - red paint for painting Ghost Dance shirts or face painting. There are 20 letters, reproduced exactly as they were found, with blank spaces inserted in areas found to be unintelligible.

They are quite interesting, considering the time of their creation, the indication being the lingering interest in the movement into the 20th century. Also evident is the continued respect for Jack Wilson implicit in the letters themselves.

46.   Dobrow, Julie. "White Sister of the Sioux." *The Masterkey for Indian Lore and History*. 56(3):103-106(1982).

The White Sister referred to here is Elaine Goodale, and this biographical sketch of her life in South Dakota is quite infomative regarding events she witnessed or situations of which she was aware. She arrived in South Dakota in 1886 to teach on the Sioux Reservation. She soon was appointed Supervisor of the schools in North and South Dakota. She learned the Sioux language, worked at learning their culture and their ways. She soon began to realize that the destruction of their world was on the horizon, due to the U.S. government taking their land in the various ways she could see it was being taken. Her writings are quoted here, her sympathies are obvious.

Her effort to teach the Indians and to learn about them resulted in the development of a deep sympathy for them and for their circumstance. She was invited to several Ghost Dances in the area. Her experiences are quoted here. Her relatively objective observations of the impact the Ghost Dance Movement was having on the Sioux, in the midst of the deterioration of their lifestyles, and of the "nervousness and panic" of the white settlers who demanded increased military protection, were written with clarity and compassion. She happened to travel to the Pine Ridge Agency in November 1890 to inspect the Ogalala boarding school, where she became aware of the mounting tension resulting from the celebration of the Ghost Dance. She also met the Sioux physician, Dr. Charles Eastman whom she later married. This article relates Goodale's experiences and her understanding of the cultural destruction perpetrated on the Sioux Nation.

47.   Eastman, Elaine Goodale. "The Ghost Dance War And Wounded Knee Massacre of 1890-91." *Nebraska History*. 26:26-42 (1945).

This an intimate memoir written by the first school teacher hired by the U.S. government for the Teton Sioux in South Dakota. This writing focuses on South Dakota and the Teton Sioux from 1885, the year of Eastman's appointment, through the Massacre in January of 1891.

The article is articulate and knowledgable about the sometimes complicated and convoluted intricacies of the U.S. government's handling of the settlement of the Sioux lands in South Dakota. Discussion of the betrayal of U.S. government promises, resulting eventually in the desperate and miserable conditons of the Sioux, is brief but explicit. The scene is set for the news of the messiah and subsequent participation in the Ghost Dance.

Eastman's position of working with the Indians on a daily basis probably was responsible for her sympathetic understanding of their situation as the days and months progressed. She recounts her conversation with Good Thunder, one of Red Cloud's messengers from the messiah, Wovoka, as well as her observations on the local military build-up, and the totally insufficient supplies and rations sent for the Sioux in the winter of 1890.

Her article includes the report of her attendance of Ghost Dances. She was in the chapel at the Pine Ridge Agency during the massacre at Wounded Knee, and was present when the wounded were brought in for medical attention.

Various versions of the incident are included in this report, from participants either in the action or in the aftermath: Eastman's report, and her quotes from the survivors of the massacre and the report of Col. Forsythe, Commander of the U.S. military force at Wounded Knee. Reports of other members of the military, Indian survivors, family members of the slain are reviewed. Reference is made to subsequent investigation into this matter immediately afterward, on-going into the twentieth century.

The paragraphs of this article are filled with facts germane to the Wounded Knee Massacre, and tell an intimate personal experience of the life of the Teton Sioux in South Dakota between 1885 and 1891.

48.   Fielder, Mildred. *Sioux Indian Leaders*.   Seattle : Superior Publishing Company, 1975.

This is a series of eight biographical sketches of some of the more influential Sioux leaders in the late 19th century. Among those biographies offered are that of Crazy Horse, Spotted Tail, Sitting Bull, Gall and Red Cloud.

The sketches contain much of the history of the Ghost Dance Movement and the participation of these men in it, the Wounded Knee Massacre, the U.S. Federal government and its other military activities.

These texts are straight-forward biographical reviews of the lives of these Sioux. Included are many portraits and photographs.

49.   Gatschet, Albert S. "Report of an Indian Visit to Jack Wilson, the Payute Messiah." *Journal of American Folklore* 6:198-111(1891).

In the autumn of 1890, three Cheyenne Indians traveled to Nevada, seeking the reputed Indian messiah. Upon returning to Montana, they reported what they found to Abe Somers, also a Cheyenne. In February, 1891, Somers recounted the tale of their experiences to Henry Dawson North, a young Arapaho in Lawrence, Kansas, who was fluent in Arapaho and Cheyenne. This is that report, as Gatschet says, "almost verbatum translated from an Indian language ."

These three Indians were Porcupine, Big Beaver and Ridge Walker. Abe Somers, the original report receiver, was not sympathetic to the Ghost Dance Movement, or this report. Nevertheless, this report contains some interesting inconsistencies. Somehow, the original message from Jack Wilson, Wovoka, claiming only to be a messenger from God, is transferred to the notion of a new Christ having arrived.

These three, traveling through Utah, are joined by many others on the same quest to find the "new Christ." Arriving at Walker Lake, they encounter the "new Christ" who instructs them in the dance, which they perform till late in the night. The next morning, this "new Christ", looking quite different, continues his instruction.

The experiences of these three are related in detail. The article concludes with a short biographic sketch of Jack Wilson (Wovoka) and his message, which is quite different from this one regarding the "new Christ."

50.   Johnson, W. Fletcher. *Life of Sitting Bull and History of the War of 1890-91.* [s.l.] : Edgwood Publications Co., 1891.

This biography of Sitting Bull and general history of the incidents in South Dakota in 1890-1891 is very detailed, if undocumented. It is written in the style of historical fiction, or a kind of historical journalism. Johnson seems, from his writing, to have been acquainted with federal officers in the military and in the Indian service.

The growth of the Ghost Dance Movement is explicitly traced through these contacts, as is the death of Sitting Bull and the involvment of Agent James P. McLaughlin. This book offers a sense of life in South Dakota in the last decades of the 19th century. The loss of Sitting Bull to his people in the midst of trying to re-establish the world as they knew it is one of the meaningful images available here.

51.   Kelley, Alexander. *Pine Ridge, 1890 : An Eye-Witness Account of the Events Surrounding the Fighting at Wounded Knee.* Edited and compiled by Alexander Kelley and Pierre Bovis. San Francisco : Pierre Bovis, 1971.

This book is a collection of newspaper articles published in the *Nebraska State Journal*, from November 24, 1890 through January 16, 1891. Kelly, along with several other newspaper reporters, was stationed at the Pine Ridge Agency during this period, and was thus witness to the rising disturbances throughout. He was on the field on December 29, 1890 during the conflict which resulted in the Wounded Knee Massacre.

These newspaper articles provide an amazingly intimate and solid chronology of the Pine Ridge Agency and of its inhabitants during this time of crippling deprivation and massive Ghost Dancing; of political and financial embezzlement, confused authority and military excess.

Also included is a group of brief biographical sketches, with portraits, of the most important characters in the drama: Gen. Nelson A. Miles, Col. John R. Brook, Red Cloud, Big Foot (Spotted Elk), Sitting Bull, Short Bull, Young-Man-Afraid-Of-His Horses, Kicking Bear and American Horse.

52.   Knight, Oliver. *Following The Indian Wars : The Story of the Newspaper Correspondents Among the Indian Campaigners.* Norman : University of Oklahoma Press, 1960.

The accounts in this book cover the reportage of accredited newspaper correspondents who reported the Indian wars between 1866 and 1891. The last major battle covered in this book is the Wounded Knee Massacre in South Dakota. Knight suggests the "newspaper coverage" of this event "marks a sharp break in the handling of Indian war news." Knight provides a brief review of the historical facts leading up to and including the military confrontation at Wounded Knee Creek. His major point, however, rests in the discussion of the changing face of the notion of news reporting.

Knight indicates the period of "basically honest reporting of army campaigns" ended with the Apache campaign in 1881. Immediatley afterward, a "New Journalism" developed typified by Joseph Pulitzer's *New York World.* This "New Journalism" was very competitive for circulation. The over-all organization was larger, human-interest writing and the quest for larger readership became such that, while accuracy was demanded in principle, in practice it often gave way to distortion for its own effect.

Knight lists the personnel included in the press corps at Wounded Knee, - 21 in all, including one woman. Only three were present at the Battle of Wounded Knee, one of these was killed. Subsequent to the actual battle, "unverified rumors became reports from reliable sources, idle gossip was reported as fact." Major distortions of the situation in South Dakota spread across the newspapers in Nebraska and the Dakotas and as far east as Iowa, causing public panic. This journalistic mayhem was brought to an end on January 15, when General Nelson A. Miles paraded the entire Seventh Battalion, partly to create a sense of awe in any Indians remaining hostile to the cavalry and partly to acknowledge the surrender of the Sioux Nation.

53.   Marshall, Julian, in collaboration with Jerome Peltier. "Wounded Knee - Battle or Tragedy?" *The Pacific Northwesterner* 23(3):41-48(1979).

Marshall, a native of the area in South Dakota near the Rosebud and Pine Ridge Reservations presents a personal narrative combined in large part with writings of others concerning the activities of the military and of the Indians there. Included is the general history of the Ghost Dance, the messiah, and the Sioux pilgrimage to Nevada. Informally quoting George Metcalf (Great Western Indian Fights), Marshall reviews the last decades of U.S. Cavalry involvement with the Indians, and the Battle of the Little Big Horn, suggesting the possibility of an 'avenging' mentality of the Seventh Cavalry. Marshall quotes newspaper articles from the Rapid City Daily Journal, December 2,8,11,12,16,17 and 23, 1890 - a key time in this history. These articles are quite specific in their reference to the Ghost Dance activities, and to their effect of these activities on the Indian participants and the white settlers in the area.

The death of Sitting Bull is related through an informal but lengthy quote from *Bury My Heart At Wounded Knee,* (Dee Brown,1972), and the actual fighting is related through a section of the 14th Annual Report of the Bureau of Ethnology, pt.2.

Perhaps the most original aspect of this article is the "Statement of John F. Hobbs," who had been in the Seventh Cavalry in South Dakota in 1890. He gave this report to Jerome Peltier in 1952, when he (Hobbs) was 84. Ordered to the Pine Ridge Agency in answer to the rising uneasiness generated by the Sioux preoccupation with the Ghost Dance, Hobbs tells his experience objectively, concerning the attempted arrest of Sitting Bull, or chasing Big Foot's band of Ghost Dancers into Paradise Valley in weather that was 30 degrees below freezing. The result is filled with intimate details and quite moving.

54.   McCoy, Tim. *Tim McCoy Remembers the West : An Autobiography.*
       Lincoln : University of Nebraska,1977,1980.

This autobiography of a flamboyant, Canadian-born 'cowboy' whose life included a long military career in the U.S. cavalry, Roosevelt's Rough Riders, and U.S. armed services in both World Wars. His time in the 19th century American West saw him in personal contact with many American Indians. He cultivated several personal relationships in the tribes with whom he was in contact, -- among them Short Bull, Kicking Bear and Yellow Knife. With their direction, he was able to seek out the Paiute Indian messiah, Wovoka, in 1924. He talked with Wovoka and arranged a Ghost Dance, apparently to see if Wovoka or the dance still carried any power. He did and it did. Nevertheless, McCoy saw Wovoka "not as one who offered (the Indians) salvation...but as a monumental factor in bringing about their destruction."

55. McGillycuddy, Julia. *McGillycuddy, Agent : A Biography of Dr. Valentine McGillycuddy*. Stanford, California : Stanford University Press, 1941.

This biography of the agent at the Pine Ridge Agency was written by his second wife, Julia. It is based largely on his oral and written reminiscences recorded in his retirement. The book treats the history of the Sioux in the process of becomming accustomed to life in ever smaller plots of land alloted to them by the U.S. government. McGillycuddy's wisdom and subtlety in dealing with the Indians under his jurisdiction is observable through the incidents related in an honest attempt to convey his life's work.

She traces his on-going trouble with the Sioux Chief, Red Cloud, his ultimate removal from Pine Ridge, his return as Adjutant General in the position of observer, the drought of 1889 and the reduction of government supplies meant for the Indians. The Wounded Knee Massacre is shown as the culmination of that segment of his life.

The book is filled with intimate personal details of the history McGillycuddy himself helped to make. His wisdom as agent is clearly unique in the midst of the so-called Indian policies and behind-the-scenes politics which prevailed and aginst which McGillicuddy was ultimately helpless.

56. McLaughlin, James. *My Friend the Indian*. Lincoln, London : University of Nebraska Press, 1910, 1989. [With 3 chapters omitted from the original ed.]

James McLaughlin made his life among the Indians, serving as Indian agent from 1871 to 1923. He worked closely with his charges, steering them into the civilized white life, helping them to build schools, and to farm. He used the power available to his office, i.e., the Indian Police, to control the more rebellious of his wards. The strongest of these was Sitting Bull. While McLaughlin worked to promote the white values like schools, farming and monogamy, attempting to direct the Indians away from their pagan dances and other customs, Sitting Bull, the powerful medicine man, "stubbornly resisted all efforts to transform him into an imitation white man and stood at the center of the opposition to [McLaughlin's] program."

This opposition from Sitting Bull became more than a nuisance to McLaughlin in the fall of 1890. When Kicking Bear returned from the people "who lived beyond the Yellow Faces to the west of the Utes," with the message of the Ghost Dance. The exact message was quoted, as well as the response, by One Bull, Sitting Bull's nephew and spy for McLaughlin at the gathering. Sitting Bull fervently embraced the new religion, and began to encourage "his people" to do the same.

McLaughlin's first move was to send his Indian Police to "eject Kicking Bear from the reservation." But the Ghost Dance Movement gained momentum and as the dances grew larger and more frequent, McLaughlin became more concerned. Finally he ordered the arrest of Sitting Bull. The death of Sitting Bull in this attempt is detailed, as well as the continued rise of the Ghost Dance in the area, culminating in the Wounded Knee Massacre.

This autobiography of McLaughlin's life among the Indians is rich in its detail of Indian life in the last decades of the 19th century, as well as its detail of the various political positions of the Indian Bureau.

57.   Moses, L.G. "'My Father Tells Me So' / Wovoka : the Ghost Dance Prophet." *American Indian Quarterly 9(3):335-351 (*Summer, 1985).

This straightforward biographical article is interesting in the detail and also in the interwoven comments of other biographers of Wovoka. In relating events of Wovoka's life, Moses uses biographical details previously related by Paul Bailey, E.A. Dyer, James Mooney, and Arthur Chapman. Combining his own scholarship with theirs', Moses traces the Ghost Dance, from January 1, 1889 through the growth of the Movement. This biography takes Wovoka's inspiration (The Ghost Dance Movement) through the Wounded Knee Massacre into the 20th century, with Col. Tim McCoy speaking to the Ghost Dance prophet in 1924.

Moses reviews Wovoka's life in terms of his being a prophet, like Paul or Joel in the bible, and in terms of the positive reality generated for the Indians by the Ghost Dance Movement.

58.   Neihardt, John G. *The Story of a Holy Man of the Oglala Sioux*. Lincoln: University of Nebraska, 1961.

The title on the title page reads as above, with the additional information: "as told to John G. Neihardt (Flaming Rainbow), illustrated by Standing Bear." John Neihardt was made poet laurete of Nebraska in 1921, and has published five volumes containing narrative poems about Indians and their lives. This book is not a poem, but a re-telling of Black Elk's life as it was told to Neihardt.

Over a period of a few months, Black Elk told his story to Neihardt. Sitting with them was Black Elk's son, who translated for Neihardt, and Neiherdt's daughter, Enid who served as stenographer.

Black Elk was present at the Wounded Knee Massacre, and the book is informative, straight forward and a very moving account of his life and times.

59.   Olson, James C. *Red Cloud and the Sioux Problem*. Lincoln : University of Nebraska, 1965.

Olson originally planned to produce a biography of the Oglala Sioux, Chief Red Cloud, using material gathered by D. Addison Sheldon, Director of the Nebraska Historical Society, over a thirty year tenure. However, Olson soon realized that what he had was experiences of Red Cloud by white men who had one problem or another with this Sioux Chief. Also, anything that was quoted from Red Cloud had been translated by an anonymous translator, or at the least, a questionably reliable translator.

This book's major focus provides an objective account of Red Cloud's role in the life of his people during the years in which they were making the transition from warriors to wards of the government. The book, with the use of statements from the "white citizens" -- farmers, military personnel, newspapermen, missionaries, etc., -- describes the "problem," as well as the stepwise destruction of the Sioux Nation, head-on.

The members of the Sioux Nation referred to are chosen from a wide spectrum of connections, and numerous points of view are represented. Many members of the Sioux Nation did not adhere to the Ghost Dance Religion, many did. Among the Sioux leaders referred to here are Red Cloud, Spotted Tail, Short Bull, Sitting Bull (Hunkpapa Chief), Sitting Bull (Oglala), Little Wound, Crazy Horse and American Horse.

60.   Overholt, Thomas W. "Short Bull, Black Elk, Sword, and the Meaning of the Ghost Dance. " *Religion* 8(2):171-195 (1978).

In this paper, Overholt observes some of the possible *meanings* avaiable to attach to the concept of the Ghost Dance as practiced by the desperate Indian tribes in the Northwest in the late 19th century. He begins by describing objectively, the Ghost Dance, its origin and its tragic outcome at Wounded Knee. The investigation into the meaning of this religious movement is begun by the qualification of "meaning for whom?" and pursued through the collected observations of whites, -- local settlers, sympathetic on-lookers, anthropologists -- and Indians.

All three of the men named in the title of this article were South Dakota Sioux. All three were holy men. However, they had widely differing attitudes toward the Ghost Dance. Short Bull was in the group who traveled to Nevada to investigate the rumor of a messiah, and was probably responsible for re-interpreting Wovoka's essentially peaceful message into one customized and more aggressive for use by the Sioux. George Sword was a progressive (co-operative with the whites) and an opponent, by-and-large, of the Ghost Dance. Black Elk was, at first, progressive, then a proponent of the Ghost Dance, and then ambivalent.

The *meaning* of the Ghost Dance is investigated through the lives of these men.

61.   Stewart, Omer C. "Contemporary Document on Wovoka (Jack Wilson) Prophet of the Ghost Dance in 1890." *Ethnohistory*. 24(3):219-222(summer, 1977).

This brief article concerns the alleged activites of Wovoka (Jack Wilson), originator of the Ghost Dance Movement, subsequent to the Wounded Knee Massacre. The main substance here consists in a report sent to Washington by Nevada Indian Agent, Inspector L.A. Dorrington, whose report describes Wovoka's life at that time, to be in true fashion, simple, that of a medicine man, who made large sums of money from "distant and more prosperous tribes" [for consultation on the continuing Ghost Dance celebration and on accompanying supplies].

Dorrington, "after careful inquiry," finds that Wovoka used no peyote or mescal, and that he actively discouraged its use among the members of his tribe.

Included is a photo of Wovoka, taken by Dorrington in 1917.

5

Anthropological Theory

62. Aberle, David. "The Prophet Dance and Reaction to White Contact."
     Southwestern Journal of Anthropology. 15:74-85(1959).

Three major points are addressed in this article, which is an informal
rejoinder to separate works and ideas promulgated by Leslie
Spier(1935), Melvill Herskovits(1938) and Wayne Suttles(1957). These
points deal with: 1) The possible effects of what is termed mediate
and/or immediate *contact*, here especially between aboriginal Indian
cultures and Euroamerican culture; 2) Contact may be obvious or it may
be more obscure. Profound cultural change may occur as a result of
either. 3) A more meaningful definition of the term deprivation is
approached.

Aberle addresses Spier's proposal that "the ultimate origin of the two
Ghost Dance Movements was...in the Northwest among the tribes of the
interior Plateau area." Spier's cultural framework suggests the origin of
what he calls the *Prophet Dance*, (a blanket term Spier coined to refer
to a similar dance performed by many Indian cultures, beginning in the
Northwest) to be aboriginal. Inherent in this theory is the absence of
white or Euroamerican contact, a phenomonon usually thought to be the
cause of cultural deterioration, or a percieved deprivation to which the
Ghost Dance has been assumed to have been a response. Spier's
assumption is that these dances had been performed long in advance of
Euroamerican contact and of the two Ghost Dances. Herskovits is
quoted to demonstrate, in agreement and even more strongly, that
"Spier has shown that neither the Ghost Dance nor the Prophet Dance
were reactions to unfavorable contact with Western culture."

Aberle responds with an enlargment of the notion of *contact* to include, in the absence of <u>direct</u> contact, the concept of " to know about" a new, strong, material culture. "We are not free to postulate contact where we know of none, but where we know that communication is possible, we are also not free to eliminate it as a possible cause of some of the events we observe."

Aberle finds at least three types of deprivation, in order to pursue the application of the concept more generally: 1) the "We are worse off than we once were" level of deprivation, denoting a perceived general worsening; 2) the "We are not as well off as they are" level, referring to another group, which could be another Indian tribe, or the whites and 3) the type which refers not to the tribe as a whole, but to individuals or possibly a group within a tribe, not being "as well off as" possibly another group within the tribe. Any or all of these conditions of relative deprivation could generate a cult response.

63.   Barber, Bernard. "Acculturation and Messianic Movements." *American Sociological Review* 6:663-669(1941).

This article is an analysis of messianic movements among the American aboriginal Indian. Barber finds twenty such movements in the United States before 1890. He also finds the conditions which usually precipitate messianic movements to be "hard times and devastation", inability to obtain what any given culture has come to expect for normal satisfaction. In the case of the American Indian, the buffalo had been a major aspect in acquisition of livelihood and shelter. The buffalo had also provided a broad base for cultural activities and ceremonies. The loss of the bullafo was devastating. The whites also introduced new diseases -- small pox, measeles, whooping cough and alcoholism.

The spread of the messianic movements depended on how "hard" the "hard times" were respectively, or how severely the deprivation cut into their culture.

Some tribes were not predisposed toward the Ghost Dance Messiah because "values of their old life still functioned." However, for tribes which faced a cultural impasse, the messianic movement "served to articulate the spiritual despair of the Indians."

Tracing the histories of the participants and the non-participants, in the Ghost Dance, Barber finds the messianic cult only one of a number of responses to this cultural deprivation. The Peyote cult is another cult, following, he supposes, disillusionment with the Ghost Dance. Acculturation happened in various ways.

64.   Carroll, Michael P. "Revitalization Movements and Social Structure: Some Quantitative Tests." *American Sociological Review* 40:389-401(June 1975).

Carroll begins by reviewing the several terms referring to "movements whose purpose [is] to radically re-structure virtually all aspects of social and cultural life," i.e., *revitalization movements*. Carroll clarifies the term (after Wallace 1925) thus: "The defining characteristic of a revitalization movement is the emphasis upon a simultaneous restructuring of virtually all social and cultural relations." Carroll proposes, in this paper, to review some of the methodological problems which lie in the path of the attempt "to develop general theories explaining the rise of such movements...."

Carroll finds that the modes of investigation into revitalization movements can be sorted into three categories: 1) those studies which "try to explain the rise of particular movements in particular cultures; 2) those which "survey a wide range of movements across a variety of cultures with an eye towards bringing out their common feature; and 3) those which occupy something of a "middle ground in restriction to a particular cultural area (if not to a particular culture) and survey a variety of movements that have all arisen in that area...." After pointing out an inherent flaw in each of these methods, Carroll suggests there is "one naturally occurring case that very closely approximates [the] experimental ideal and that case concerns the spread of the Ghost Dance Religion among the Indian tribes of North America at the end of the last century." An explanation of this religion is followed by a brief review of the major work done on this topic by James Mooney. Using Mooney's lists of tribes -- aware of / not aware of the Ghost Dance -- participating and / not participating / -- Carroll cross-references these lists with Murdock's *Ethnographic Atlas* (1967) to establish a sample group of 37 tribes, 12 of which fall into the area categorized as low acceptance of the Ghost Dance, the remaining 25 into the group of "relatively high acceptance."

With these 37 tribes, Carroll then investigates the following relationships: distance between tribe and the source of the Ghost Dance (Walker Lake, Nevada), and acceptance; recency of the loss of the buffalo and acceptance of the Ghost Dance; number of jurisdictional levels above the local level and acceptance of the Ghost Dance; presence of unilateral kin groups and acceptance of the Ghost Dance; and presence of inheritance system and acceptance of the Ghost Dance.

Only one of Carroll's initial predictions was supported by the data: that "acceptance of the Ghost Dance should have been higher among those tribes most recently deprived as a result of the extermination of the buffalo...." His contribution here "has been to make more visible the methodological advantages of studying the Ghost Dance."

65.   Carroll, Michael P. "Rejoinder to Landsman" *American Sociological Review.44(1):*166-168(1979).

Carroll's "Rejoinder" to G. Landsman's "Response to Carroll"(ASR,1979) concerns several "methodological errors" in her remarks. His original hypothesis was based on this fact: if a society has a social structure which provides a strong sense of attachment, such a society would be less likely to accept a revitalization movement like the Ghost Dance. "Assuming that unilineal descent groups promoted this sense of attachment," the prediction was made that the presence of such groups would produce a low rate of acceptance of these movements. The original data supported this prediction.

The tribes which Landsman cites as already involved in different revitalization movements (the Peyote Cult and the Smohalla Cult) therefore should be classified, not in the low acceptance group, but in the high acceptance group. For one thing, three of these tribes, the Commanche, Mescalero Apache and Nez Perce, lack unilineal descent groups. Therefore, the original hypothesis predicts they should have been in the high acceptance group. Carroll points out this reclassification "would weaken the suport for the other hypothesis," involving relative deprivation. This is the view most frequently espoused in the literature on revitalization. The acknowledgment of unilineal decent as an aspect of a group's acceptance of a revitalization movement is Carroll's contribution.

The initial proposal in Carroll's article concerns acceptance of the Ghost Dance, as a revitalization movement. The Smohalla Cult and the Peyote Cult are questionable references for inclusion in the construction of this sample, as is the reference to the Land Allotment Act. The Smohalla Cult involved over thirty tribes, scattered thoughout the Columbia River

Basin, none of which were included in Carroll's original sample, because they were not involved in the Ghost Dance. Mooney reports "that Smohalla himself knew about the land allotment laws...and regarded land allotment as contrary to Indian cosmology." With regard to the Peyote Cults, and regarding six of the cultures in Landsman's sample, the cult began to flourish only *after* the year land allotment was established for that culture.

Landsman lists five tribes for which land was allotted before 1889. All five are unilineal descent groups, the obvious early targets for allotment laws and policies. Only one tribe had a high acceptance of the Ghost Dance.

66.   DeMallie, Raymond J. "The Lakota Ghost Dance : An Ethnohistorical Account." *Pacific Historical Review* 51(4):385-405(1982).

DeMallie reviews studies of the Ghost Dance with respect to the authors' points of view. DeMallie finds that the works of James P. Boyd, *Recent Indian Wars*,(1891) and W. Fletcher Johnson, *Sitting Bull and the Indian War of 1890-91*,(1891), provide a great deal of historical material, but having been drawn primarily from newspaper sources, also dwell on the sensational aspects of the events. James Mooney's anthropological classic, *The Ghost Dance Religion and the Sioux Outbreak of 1890*(1896), stresses the "revivalistic aspects" of the Ghost Dance, and the hope it offered for cultural regeneration. Later works done on the Sioux Ghost Dance have, in DeMallie's view, focused "either on the Indian or the military point of view." George Hyde's *A Sioux Chronical*(1956) is an attempt to "reconcile both perspectives," and to reveal the policital and economic context of the Ghost Dance. DeMallie offers Robert M. Utley's *The Last Days of the Sioux Nation* as the "definitive study" and the best description of the "military perspective."

The Sioux acceptance of the Ghost Dance has been "interpreted as a response to the stress caused by military defeat, the disappearance of the buffalo, and confinement on a reservation." The Ghost Dance religion itself has been considered to have been generated by social and political unrest. Dr. Valentine McGillycuddy, "former dictatorial agent of Pine Ridge, diagnosed the situation in January 1891: 'As for the ghost dance, too much attention has been paid to it. It was only the symptom or surface indication of deep-rooted, long existing difficulty....'" (Mooney, 1896). DeMallie cites other, alternate references to the 'hostile' nature of the Sioux version of the Ghost Dance: "...brought to the edge of starvation by reduction of rations, the doctrine speedily assumed a hostile meaning." (Mooney,1896). Robert Lowie, in the "standard text" *Indians of the Plains*, states "...the disciples of Wovoka in the Plains substituted for his policy of amity a holy war in which the Whites were to be exterminated."

DeMallie feels these analyses have "become standard in the writings of both historians and anthropologists." He re-evaluates here, with these observations, clarifying some of the fundamental aspects inherent in the previous works. First, he feels most of the literature on the Ghost Dance, assuming the Sioux assimilated the Ghost Dance from the Paiutes, underestimates the "vast cultural differences between the two tribes." Second, the assumption that the Sioux "perverted into violence" the doctrine of the Ghost Dance "implies that the Lakota Ghost Dance religion was characterized by a unified body of doctrinal teaching." Accounts of visits with Wovoka, the prophet, imply each man went away with a personal interpretation. For the Sioux, this was consistent with traditional practices, which left the individual free to contribute to the overall understanding of religious power through his own experiences. Third, the analysis asserts the leaders or messengers of the Ghost Dance Movement misled their followers for political reasons. This assumes that to its leaders, the Ghost Dance was a political movement under the pretense of religion. Fourth, the implication that the Sioux "threw themselves wholeheartedly into the ritual" implies "irrational fanaticism." Evidence shows the Sioux participation in the Ghost Dance to have been limited to the fall and early winter of 1890, and that the majority of the participants in the Ghost Dance camps were congregated out of fear of the large military presence in the area. That is why they ultimately attempted to flee to the badlands.

DeMallie's position is that the reasons the "previous historical analyses of the Lakota Ghost Dance have been inadquate lie in our reluctance to consider seriously the symbolic content of Indian cultures -- in this instance, to allow the Lakotas their own legitimate perspective." The perspective of the Lakota, for example, "was set in the interrelatedness of man, animals, earth, even plants which the white man either did not acknowledge or did not take seriously." The Lakota attributed the disappearance of the buffalo to the white man. They also "thought of the land, the animals, and the people as a single system, no part of which could change without affecting the others."

DeMallie proposes to use a "more general theoretical perspective that may profitably be applied to ethnohistorical study -- namely, *symbolic anthropology*. This method attempts to isolate differing significant symbols -- units of meaning -- that define perspectives on reality within different cultural systems." "This does not reduce history to ideological conflicts, but uses ideology to understand the motivation that underlies behavior."

67. Dobyns, Henry F. and Robert C. Euler. *The Ghost Dance of 1889 Among the Pai Indians of Northwestern Arizona*. Flagstaff, Arizona : Prescott College Press, 1967.

This work is a study of the Ghost Dance among the Walapai and Hovasupai Indians of the southwest in the 1880's and 1890's. A conscientious systhesis is achieved of Pai Ghost Dance participants' statements acquired betweeen 1910 and 1915, of newpaper reports contemporary with these events and of the authors' interviews with the tribal members in the 1950's.

The balance between eye-witness accounts, the historian's approach and the approach of the ethnographer is one main concern in this work. Another is the near destruction of the Pai people altogether in the 1860's in their first encounter with Europeans. The destruction of the religion, which accompanied this phase of their history left the Pai open to the 'messiah craze' twenty years later. These events are traced specifically and verified through Pai informants.

68. Dorsey, James P. *A Study of Siouan Cults*. 1894; [Seattle : Shorey Book Store, 1972 reprint].

This is a comprehensive study of Sioux religion and culture, the material for which was compiled by Dorsey, a missionary to the Ponka Indians in Nebraska from 1871 to 1873. He has included here information "from native texts" from the Omaha, Ponka, Osage, Kansa, Winnebago, Iowa, Oto, Missouri and Dakota tribes. Based on interviews with tribal informants, Dorsey has collected explicit information on the cults of the Sioux, defining a *cult* as a "system of religious beliefs and worship, especial'y the rites and ceremonies employed in such worship." Also included are selections of myths, along with a discussion of the difference between a myth / legend and the superhuman. This treatment of the specific features of the Sioux religion is presented with hand-executed illustrative material accompanying the text.

Linguistic information provided is based on the alphabet adopted by the Bureau of Ethnology, and Dorsey devotes several pages to translating songs and rites from the Sioux, as well as many transliterated texts on the ceremonies. The issue of names as well as their acquisition is also treated linguistically.

There are large sections dealing with ghosts, the dead, relations with the dead, and the attendant ceremonies. However, on last page, the author submits this paragraph: "Since the present article was begun there had arisen the so-called 'Messiah craze' among the Dakota and other tribes of Indians. The author does not feel competent to describe this new form of Indian religion, but he suspects that some features of it are either "willful or accidental perversions of the teachings of missionaries."

69.   DuBois, Cora. "The 1870 Ghost Dance." University of California *Anthropological Records*. 3(1):131 pages(1939).

This is an anthropological study tracing the introduction and the subsequent course of the 1870 Ghost Dance in northern California. DuBois' study is tribe specific, indicating the exact point of contact with the Ghost Dance, and the ceremonial aspects transmitted from one small tribe (she coins the word 'tribelet') to another.

She used 140 informants in her investigation, but only specifies 101 of them in her report. She lists the informants she used by name, with a small paragraph citing their usefullness as informants: for example, "needs an interpreter," or "clear-minded" or "co-operative but only moderately informed." She points out in the introduction that, in the 1930's, an informant would necessarily be 70 or 80 years old. In addition, she discovered that most of the information she received regarding participation in the Ghost Dance was not autobiographical, but biographical. The participating informants were unwilling to discuss their own experiences.

The course of the 1870 Ghost Dance is detailed in this work which discusses participation of 33 tribes or tribelets. Also included are maps of the village to village movement of the Ghost Dance and its off-shoots, which are also detailed here. They include the Big-Head Cult, the Earth Lodge Cult and the Bole-Maru Cults. There are also diagrams of the dance steps and illustrations of the clothing and other religious paraphernalia used in the dances.

70. Gayton, A.H. "The Ghost Dance of 1870 in South-Central California." *University of California Publications in Archeology and Ethnology.* 28:58-72(1930).

This is a detailed description of the spread of the Ghost Dance from 1870 through 1875 among the Yokuts and Western Mono tribes in south-central California, through the San Joaquin Valley and into Pleasanton. In addition, the study includes a well substantiated description of the pertinent cultures here, and some of their extant religious ceremonies before the infusion of the Ghost Dance Movement, which are compared to some of the salient features of the Ghost Dance.

Gayton details the spread of the Ghost Dance Movement, locating the several individuals responsible for the transmission of the news of this new religious movement. A Northern Paiute missionary first came to a Western Mono group living on the North Fork of the San Joaquin River. Joijoi, a chief there became an enthusiastic proselytizer of this new religion, carrying this message to the "foothill Mono and Yakut tribes as far south as Mill Creek and the Kings River...." Joijoi sponsored a huge dance at Saganiu in May, 1871. The many attendants of this initial dance began to spread the message. Other specific individuals who actively took it upon themselves to spread the Ghost Dance message were Inolya, a Yaudanchi messenger, and Watcilala, a Wakehummi messenger. Gayton details two large Ghost Dances: the one at Saganiu and the one held at Eshom Valley. Included are descriptions of the actual dance steps of the dance, patterns of face paint (diagramed), clothing and ceremonial feathers and headresses, and some lyrics to the songs.

The features of the Ghost Dance which were already indigenous "cultural forms" were: the "father" identified as the creator; assumption of possible contact with the dead, possible movement into and out of the land of the dead; bathing in the morning; use of standard face paint patterns; six-day ritual; taboo on sleep.

71. Gifford, Edward Winslow. "Southern Maidu Religious Ceremonies." *American Anthropologist* n.s.29(3):214-257(1927).

Gifford bases his investigations on work done by A.L. Kroeber in California, on the designation of these four basic cults : the New Year cult, the Kuksu or God-impersonating cult, the Jimsonweed cult, and the Dream cult. Kroeber had also outlined the geographic relationships between them. This paper deals with the God-impersonating cult or the Kuksu cult, located in central California among the Patwin of the lower-Sacremento valley. "To date the fullest published knowledge on the Kuksu cult concerns the Northwest Maidu, the Patwin and the Pomo."

This paper draws the various distinctions in their relationship to the personage or deity of Kuksu among the individual tribes in this area: the Pomo - Yuki held him to be the god of the south; to the Northwestern Maidu he was the first man; to the Miwok he was a "sylvan [i.e. forest or tree] spirit." "Among the Patwin and Northwestern Maidu the Kuksu impersonator did not dance or form the central figure of a ceremony. Kroeber had suggested the Patwin and the Maidu, although centrally located in the Sacramento valley, celebrated what came to be an aberrant form, the celebrations of border tribes being the most representative. "The Maidu and Patwin once shared the generalized or Pomo-Yuki-Miwok form of the cult, perhaps even originated it. Either because of this earlier start, however, or because of a more rapid progression, they developed the generalized form of the system to its limits and then passed beyond it to their own peculiar *Hesi-Moki* form, leaving the outer tribes, such as the Pomo and Miwok, adhering to the older rites...."

Gifford investigates the southernmost Southern Maidu in this paper, revealing "the relation of the ceremonialism of the Southern Maidu to that of their northwestern congeners and their other central Californian neighbors, the Patwin and the Miwok."   Gifford's "purpose of determining the ceremonial relations of the Southern Maidu" is well accomplished. The numerous tribes and their specific relationships to the ceremonies, referred to as Kusku or God-impersonating cult, are described and delineated, with respect to these ceremonies and to the possible acquisition of the ceremonies. The introduction of the Ghost Dance in 1872, by an Indian named Yoktco among the Southern Maidu, may have brought with it the element of dreaming, although "there is no certainty, since nothing is known as to whether or not dreams played a part in the older stratum of dances. However, dreaming on the part of the *temaya* or dance director strongly suggests the similar phenomenon among the so-called *Maru* priests of the Ghost Dance Cult among the Pomo." Gifford also says "As far south as Madera county an informant spontaneously told me that the names of Southern Miwok dances were the names of dead people, exactly as did a Southern Maidu informant. If this concept is not connected with the 1872 Ghost Dance, then it seems likely that it is an ancient concept that characterized the God-impersonating cult. Ghost impersonations were a marked feature of the old cult among the Pomo."

72.   Halpern, Abraham M. *Southeastern Pomo Ceremonials : The Kuksu Cult and Its Successors.* Berkeley, Los Angeles and London : University of California, 1987. [University of California Publications : Anthropological Records; v. 29]

Based on material gathered in 1936 and 1937, this manuscript, originally produced by Abraham Halpern (here edited by Katherine Spencer Halpern) is an investigation into the original Kuksu Cult. Halpern was interested in specific details of the cult, discovering how the Kuksu, the Ghost Dance Movement, the Big Head, the Earth Lodge and the Bole-Maru Cults are related to each other and where they fit into the Pomo Indian culture.

Halpern based his information primarily on statements made by five informants, all of whom were 65 years old or older in 1936-37.

73.   Herskovits, Melville J. *Acculturation : The Study of Culture Contact.* Gloucester, MA : Peter Smith, 1958.

The contribution of this ethnologist to the study of the Ghost Dance is in the realm of investigation into the nature of the movement itself, i.e. locating its origin, and determining the appropriate applications of the respective notions of *acculturation, assimilation* and *revitalization.*

Herskovits begins by reviewing the several approaches to the definition of *acculturation* available through other ethnologists. In addition, he undertakes to present his own more formal and rigorous approach to the question of acculturation. In the "Outline for the Study of Acculturation," prepared by the Sub-Committee of the Social Science Research Council (Redfield, Linton, and Herskovits,1936) he states: "Acculturation comprehends those phenomena which result when groups of individuals having different cultures come into continuous first-hand contact, with subsequent changes in the original cultural patterns of either or both groups."

His investigation of acculturation initially consists of reviewing the conclusions of other anthropologists on this issue, with whom he is in agreement. He examines the studies of Leslie Spier in a representative work, *The Prophet Dance of the Northwest*(1935). Spier's theory is that the Ghost Dance was a continuation of religious cultural facets, initially begun in tribes in the Northwest, earlier than either of the Ghost Dances, and probably also as a result of some kind of deprivation. This position, taken by Spier and Herskovits, is supported later in this review by Spier's reference to the evidence of a small group of Iroquois from Quebec, relocating themselves among the Flathead in Montana. These Iroquois had been in immediate contact with Catholicism in their former home, and they "introduced their new neighbors to the concepts and practices of Catholicism." Spier locates some of these [Catholic] "concepts and practices" in both of the subsequent Ghost Dances. Herskovits continues this discussion, citing Spier's references to the Smohalla cult, the Shaker religion, also based in variant forms of Christianity.

In addition, other approaches to the question of the fundamental origin of the Ghost Dance are presented : A.H. Gayton's discussion of the spread of the 1870 Ghost Dance into south-central California, and Phileo Nash's concern with the issue of acculturation, enlarged in scope to include such movements in New Guinea and India, as well as in North America. Hershovits feels Nash over-emphasizes the impact on the Indians of white contact, and finds it "regrettable" that Nash uses the term *acculturation* exclusively with reference to "adaptation to white modes of life."

A discussion of Alexander Lesser's *The Pawnee Ghost Dance Hand Game* is presented. Lesser stated, "...their old life was gone, and nothing adequate had been given them in its place." "[The Ghost Dance] promised the coming of a new and restored Indian earth, on which the white man would be no more, and on which the buffalo would roam again." It included as another of its tenets, the casting aside of the white man's ways, as a demonstration of faith. With its third tenet, the concern with visions and the encouragement to seek them, came "moments of intercommunication between those here on earth and their deceased kinsmen in the beyond." Thus, for the Pawnee, the Ghost Dance was one of *revitalization,* a "contra-acculturative" movement, with its fundamental roots lodged deeply in the aboriginal pattern.

Herskovits also evaluates other ethnologists' works addressing other movements of primitive groups, with motivations similar to those of the Ghost Dance Movement participants.

74.   Hertzberg, Hazel W. *The Search for an American Indian Identity :
      Modern Pan-Indian Movements.* [Syracuse] : Syracuse University Press,
      1971.

      Hertzberg discusses religious *pan-Indianism* beginning in the 19th
      century with prophetic and messianic movements among the Delaware
      and Shawnee, but none as widespread as the Ghost Dance of the late
      1880's and 1890's. Description of this movement is followed by a
      comparison of the Ghost Dance religion and the Peyote cult, its followers
      and adherents. Identifying the Ghost Dance as one of several beginning
      pan-Indian movements, Hertzberg discusses the original Ghost Dance
      in detail, as well as the somewhat changed version as it was practiced
      in South Dakota.

      The theme of this book is found in the notion of Pan-Indianism and its
      progress in the 20th century.

75.   Hill, W.W. "The Navaho Indians and the Ghost Dance of 1890."
      American Anthropologist N.S.46:523-527(1944).

      Hill begins by tracing the various possible avenues through which the
      Navaho might have become acquainted with the message of the 1890
      Ghost Dance Religion. He then discusses the specific aspects of the
      movement regarding which this New Mexico tribe were informed,
      probably through the Southern Ute tribes in Northwest New Mexico.
      Hill states "It is clear that the Navaho were thoroughly cognizant of all
      the essential elements of the Ghost Dance of 1890." What is addressed
      here is "...why the Navaho failed to embrace a doctrine found palatable
      by so many Indian peoples of North America...."

      Hill reviews several suggestions for the answer to this question:
      Barber's answer which rests in the Navaho's lack of social and spiritual
      'deprivation,' and in the fact that their [the Navaho's] "life was
      integrated around a stable culture pattern" and Wisler's, which links the
      spread of the Ghost Dance to the Plains and the cultural vacuum there.
      Hill presents his view, which is substantiated by appended statements
      of eight Navaho informants, which revealed the major reason for the
      rejection of the Ghost Dance was the fear of the dead, fundamental to
      their culture. This fear overshadowed the lure of any potential benefits
      offered by the Ghost Dance.

76.   Hittman, Michael. "The 1870 Ghost Dance at the Walker River Reservation : A Reconstruction." *Ethnohistory* 20(3):247-278(summer 1973).

This is a review of some of the available scholarship concerning the real nature of the Ghost Dance phenomenon. These studies discuss the movement as either an on-going aspect of religious ceremonial life in this area (and other adjacent areas), consistent with Basin-Plateau culture, purported so by Leslie Spier and, subsequently Cora DuBois, or, as suggested by Hittman, a religious movement "whose genesis lies in the socio-economic deprivation suffered by the participating Indians." Hittman finds the 1870 Ghost Dance Movement in Nevada to be a transformative one -- to change life back into life as it was before the incursion of Euroamerican expansion.

The specific destruction of the life of the Paviotso tribes is outlined -- the loss of their land and their food supply, epidemics, drought, and the failed promises from the U.S. government. These facts are traced through summarizing the Annual Reports of the Commissioner of Indian Affairs (ARCIA), for the years 1858-1872.

Hittman also discusses the distinction between Wodziwob, the leader and prophet of the 1870 Ghost Dance, (a parallel is drawn with Wovoka), and Wodziwob the shaman, a function he (and Wovoka) performed after the Ghost Dance Movement had ended. This discussion defining the 'shaman' figure serves to aid in the distinction between the *on-going-religion* theory and the special position and/or *need* for the Ghost Dance.

Hittman's other major point in this paper is the unique aspect of the Ghost Dance regarding the resurrection of the dead. The Paviotso practiced a "ritual avoidance" of the dead, but the degree of destruction of their culture, along with the massive reduction of their population was so great, the Movement continued to grow until the specified date for resurrection passed. Then, interest in the Ghost Dance began to decline. It was then Wodziwob went on to become a shaman or doctor.

77.   Hittman, Michael. "Ghost Dances, Disillusionment and Opiate Addiction: An Ethnohistory of Smith and Mason Valley." Ph.D. diss., University of New Mexico, 1973. [Diss. Ab. #v./343/10-B] Reprint. Ann Arbor, MI : University Microfilms, 1973.

This study investigates the ethnohistorical question, "Did disillusionmemt follow the 1870 or 1890 Ghost Dance, and if so, can disillusionment explain Smith and Mason Valley Paiute opiate addiction."

Hittman makes the distinction between the Ghost Dance Movements of 1870 and 1890 in Nevada to be quite specific: the 1870 Movement was coincident with "absolute deprivation," a condition which caused the Paiute to accept the promise of Wodziwob to resurrect the dead and to overcome their basic fear of the dead. This movment "functioned as a transformative one, and came to an abrupt end when Wodziwob failed to resurrect lost family members and friends.

The 1890 Movement in Nevada was not predicated on massive deprivation, but on the charismatic originator, Wovoka, (Jack Wilson). This movement, with a higher profile than the earlier one, due to the pilgrims from many other states in which there was major deprivation, was, for the Paiute, a redemptive one.

Within a few years of the abandonment of the 1890 Ghost Dance Movement in Nevada, opiate addiction began there. Hittman's explanation for this addiction focuses on "loss of traditional Paiute culture, directed culture change via schools and churches, basic demographic transition," and several other factors.

Hittman's fourth chapter, "The 1870 and 1890 Ghost Dances" discusses the various anthropological theories advanced in that field concerning the nature of the Ghost Dance, and its "real" origin. He traces, through his own investigations in Nevada, the lives and histories of the prophets of both movements, and he includes here an impressive amount of detailed fact. An interesting device employed is his use of the footnote. The on-going text is comprehensive and well organized. The section of footnotes at the end of each chapter, however provides another level of the essence of these facts. Here we read, for example, that the man called Tavibo (Wovoka's father) or 'Niniraivo?O', Paiute-White man, even though he was not a half-breed, did not die until 1910. Thus, Wovoka was not an orphan. Also, the footnotes address the Spier-DuBois-Walker-(etc.) Prophet Dance vs. Deprivation/Revitalization/(etc.) issue, relating comments in the text to these theories.

This is one of the major works on this subject, written with depth of perception, with affection for the Ghost Dance participants and for other scholars of the Movement.

78.   Jorgensen, Joseph G. "Ghost Dance, Bear Dance, and Sun Dance."
       Handbook of North American Indians, V.11, The Great Basin. Edited by
       Warren L. D'Azevedo. Washington, D.C. : Smithsonian Institution, 1969.

       Jorgensen traces the origin of the Ghost Dance from Wodziwob, a
       northern Piute from the Walker Lake region of Nevada. The devastation
       of the Piute tribes through the 1860's and 1870's is found responsible for
       the spread of the Ghost Dance idea throughout the Great Basin region.

       Jorgensen finds the major thrust of Wodziwob's Ghost Dance in 1869 to
       be transformative, i.e. to change, immediately the lives the Indians had
       been forced into; to bring back all deceased family and friends; to be rid
       of the white man and bring back all the buffalo. This movement began
       in Nevada, spread to California and somewhat to Oregon, but was
       relatively short lived. It was ended, by and large, by 1872.

79.   Kehoe, Alice Beck. *The Ghost Dance : Ethnohistory And Revitalization.*
       New York : Holt, Rinehart and Winston, 1989.

       This book is divided into two parts. The first chapters are primarily
       ethnohistorical. Kehoe traces the Ghost Dance Movement, including
       description of Wovoka's father, Tavibo, Wovoka's childhood (age 14-)
       with the Wilson family and the beginning of his religious experience,
       starting with the total eclipse in January, 1889. This historical review
       outlines Wovoka's original notions of pacifism and of leading the "clean
       and honest life." The spread of the Ghost Dance Movement from the
       Paiutes in Nevada is traced to the Indian tribes throughout the
       Southwest and California, and to the Northwest. Here Wovoka's original
       ideas were greatly re-interpreted. Also traced is the systematic
       reclamation of Indian reservations by the U.S. government under
       President Harrison.

       Special incidents of the Ghost Dance Movement are outlined and the
       U.S. government response to it are presented, the respective
       developments indicating a course of collision. A chapter is given over to
       Black Elk, an eloquent and thoughtful Oglala Sioux medicine man.

       Chapter six is a review of the second confrontation between Indians and
       armed federal troops at Wounded Knee Creek, in South Dakota, in
       February, 1973. A comparison of it and the first one in 1890-1891 is
       drawn, followed by an historical outline through the 20th century

pointing to the on-going lack of consistent relationship between the U.S. government and the American Indian.

80.   Kroeber, A.L. "A Ghost Dance in California. *The Journal of American Folk-Lore.* 17(64):31-35(January-March 1904).

This ethnological delineation of the Ghost Dance in northern California traces the growth and the development of this religious movement among the Yurok and Karok Indians of the lower Klamath river. An old Tolowa started the movement near the coast in this region. He and his nephew, a Yurok, "learned to dream" and proceeded to teach their methods of experiencing the dreams and the dance. They became the major proselytizers of the discipline, 'dreamed', interpreted their dreams for the various tribes and became prophets of the movement.

Kroeber describes the dance itself, the form of which seems to have remained consistent in its communication from one tribe to another: concentric circles, revolving in alternate directions, and as large as 10 such circles. The main feature of the Ghost Dance here was the return of the dead. The village to village contact with the Ghost Dance is traced, as well as the mores, idiosyncratic to this area. For example, "all dogs were killed." "Valuables kept secreted would be lost." "Men and women were ordered to bathe together without shame, and did so. Sexual intercourse was forbidden." There were many more, many of which -- but not all -- were already common in the local ceremonies.

81.   Kroeber, A.L. *Handbook Of The Indians Of California.* New York : Dover Publications, 1925, 1976.

Kroeber has compiled a work of authoritative dimensions (995 pages) in this description of the physical - cultural - religious make-up of some fifty tribes or little nations. The work is arranged, as Kroeber states, by tribes, "...picturing as concretely as I might, the customs of each ...adding discussions and comparisons of broader scope wherever the knowledge in hand made such procedure profitable." Kroeber does not organize the material in an historical approach. Regarding the fluctuation of population, since all statistics date from a late date, only the effect of "Caucasian contact" is pursued. "The disintegration of native numbers and native culture have proceeded hand in hand, but in very different ratios according to locality. The relationship between the type of culture and the density of the population is nearly always significant." Archeological discussion has been kept to a minimum, as well as that of physical types. Investigation into the province of speech has been entertained "only in so far as the accumulating knowledge of the languages of California has led to their classification on a genetic or historical basis and thus contributes to the insight of the origin, movements, and relationship of the several nations." Music is the one cultural activity Kroeber has treated only incidently, due to the size of the subject and ..."to have included it on an unsuperficial basis would have entailed a section of disproportionate size."

The organization of this book relies heavily on three indexes: "Classification of Titles by Subject, with the sub-groups, e.g., Archaeology, Ethnology - Topical, Ethnology - Tribal, etc; Classified Subject Index; and General Index, which is arranged according to tribal name. Each section, treating the individual tribes is ended with a "conclusion" or summary.

The Ghost Dance "which swept northern California with some vehemence from about 1871 to 1873 or 1874" is treated in individual discussion of the tribes, as well as in a separate section. The movement of 1889 and 1890 left California untouched. Kroeber discusses the movement briefly, and traces its spread in the north among the Karok and the Tolowa. Further south, the tribes involved were the Pomo and southern and central Wintun, the Yokuts and the Modoc, the Shasta, the Yana, the Maidu and Klamuth tribes. This is accompanied by a map showing the spread of and involvement with the Ghost Dance.

82.   Landsman, Gail. "The Land Allotment Policy." *American Sociological Review* 44(1):162-163(1979).

Landsman introduces her topic, the Land Allotment Policy, by discussing a work by Michael P. Carroll (ASR June,1975). Carroll "uses the case of the Ghost Dance to test quantitatively, hypotheses derived from various theories on the rise and acceptance of revitalization movements." Two prerequisites are suggested: recent deprivation and the absence of unilineal kin groups. Landsman submits that deprivation, being applicable in most cases of culture contact, does not reveal how and when "mobilization into a social movement takes place. Nor does it allow for much depth in the analysis of the effects of government policy on the rise and spread of movements."

Landsman takes exception with Carroll's sample of tribes "dichotomized on the basis of high and low acceptance of the Ghost Dance." Landsman establishes that two of the tribes in the "low acceptance" group were already "involved in other revitalization movements, i.e. the Peyote cult and the Smoholla cult. The "Hopi as well were organized in both passive and active resistance." In addition, Landsman documents the fact that it is unlikely the Jicarilla Apache even knew about the Ghost Dance. Landsman goes on to review Carroll's discussion of two major theories of social movements. The first concerns the "role of *relative deprivation.*" The second involves "the correlation between acceptance of revitalization movements [like the Ghost Dance] and a given society's level of integration, i.e., the degree to which an individual feels a sense of solidarity with some social group." (Carroll,1975:397) Carroll offers two propositions which ensue from the second theory referred to above. This theory is referred to by Landsman as the "mass society theory of social movements." These are 1) extremist social movements are most likely to flourish in societies in which few people participate in associations. 2) It is the alienated and atomized individuals who make up the ranks of such movements." Carroll suggests that acceptance of a revitalization movement is a response to a lack of cohesion within the groups that compose the society. Landsman proposes to test this "integration argument" by "examining the effects of the allotment of land in severalty, a legislative policy designed to destroy the tribal cohesion of American Indian societies."

Pressure for the Land Allotment Policy came from white settlers, as well as lumber, mining and railroad interests who hoped to gain "access to the surplus lands," on the one hand. On the other, "philanthropists" hoped private ownership of an individual piece of land would produce a civilizing effect on the Indians. Landsman describes the Land Allotment Policy, generated by the Dawes Act, enacted in 1887. It involved 160 acres of land for each head of family, with lesser amounts of land allotted to individuals. These allotments were held in trust by the U.S. government for 25 years, in order to protect the lands from land-greedy speculators. Choice of allotment was to be made within 4 years, citizenship was to be conferred on allotees, and on all other Indians who had abandoned their tribes. "Lands left over after individual allotments had been assigned were to be opened up to white settlement." The goal of this legislation's promoters was to do away with tribalism and community ownership of lands, with the concentration of Indians on reservations, with Indian religious rites and cultural patterns. Dawes himself explained that the idea of allotment was: "to take the Indians out one by one from under the tribe, place him in a position to become an independent American citizen, and then before the tribe is aware of it, its existence as a tribe is gone." The figures that follow in the paper demonstrate that the transfer of land ownership from Indians to whites resulted in the lands held by Indians having been cut in half by 1900.

Landsman then proceeds to discuss the relationship of acceptance of the Ghost Dance among tribes whose members accepted allotments, and those who, for various reasons, were not allotted or were offered allotments after 1889. The evidence demonstrates a high correlation between land allotment and low acceptance of a revitalization movement. The policy of the government seems to have worked. "Keeping a population physically separated so that no sense of common interest or solidarity can easily develop may be regarded as a way of preventing potential partisans from organizing." Landsman observes that the general literature on the effects of allotment of land in severalty reveals "...that allotment was failing and that contrasts between tribal and allotted land use patterns revealed how the latter was destroying tribal life and creating indigent and landless Indians."(Sutton,1975)

83.   Lesser, Alexander. "The Cultural Significance of the Ghost Dance." *American Anthropologist* n.s.35:108-115(1933).

Lesser's investigation into the general cultural significance the Ghost Dance Movement carried for the Indian is pursued through the relevant facts available in the observation of the Pawnee tribe, assuming these to be consistently applicable to the Indian plight in general. Lesser traces the decline of the Pawnee culture, along with that of the rest of the Indians due to the domination of the white man. With it came the decline of stimulus for the elder generation to teach the younger the ritual lessons necessary for its replacement. In the case of the Pawnee, knowldege regarding ceremonial "bundles" of sacred paraphernalia was also necessary, in addition to lessons in the performance of sacred rites and ceremonies. The ultimate demise of the culture was on the horizon, with the death of the priests, the carriers of the cultural seeds. Lesser counts this element among the loss of the land, the massive influx of white settlers, and the loss of the buffalo to be the major decisive feature of the demise of the life of the Indian.

The Ghost Dance offered salvation from this morass. The Indian ways were not irretrievably gone! All the promises of the Ghost Dance were like a ray of bright sun. In addition, the dances themselves offered 'communication' with the elders from beyond. The Pawnee could again celebrate their rites and ceremonies. The 'memories' were rekindled through the trances of the Ghost Dance, through its celebration. This advantge also offered tacit community consent and respect to unofficial expertise, without the formal training by an acknowledged priest. In this way, the Ghost Dance was a *revival* movement, inspiring its disciples to reintegrate the meaningful aspects of their old ways into their lives, "for an actual renaissance of the forms of old culture."

84.   Linton, Ralph. "Nativistic Movements." *American Anthropologist* 45:230-240(1943).

This is an investigation into the notion of *nativistic movements,* initially devised to address the study of nativistic phenomena in general and specifically, the study of the effects of acculturation. Linton first defines the term nativistic movements as "any conscious, organized attempt on the part of a society's members to revive or perpetuate selected aspects of its culture." After some discussion, he delineates the problem into four possible aspects:

1. Revivalistic-Magical -- the attempt to revive aspects of the culture feared to be lost, through spectacular methods.

2. Revivalistic-Rational -- the attempt to revive these desired aspects through non-magical means.

3. Perpetuative-Magical -- the attempt to perpetuate what currently is in the culture through magical methods (Linton admits he has been unable to find any clearly recognizable example of this aspect.)

4. Perpetuative-Rational -- the attempt to perpetuate what currently is through rational means.

Linton acknowledges that these four forms of nativistic movements are not absolute, and that they are not mutually exclusive. The American Indian Ghost Dance Movement is a perfect example for his discussion of the practicability of reviving or perpetuating distinctive elements of the cultures of the participating tribes. He also refers to "distinctive Ghost Dance 'art' (possibly Ghost Dance shirts, or paint) as "new elements of culture [which] often emerge in connection with magical [messianic] nativistic movements."

This is an important anthropological inquiry, ultimately into the overall understanding of the process of *acculturation*, a part of which is, as defined by Linton, nativistic movements.

85.   Logan, Brad. "The Ghost Dance Among the Paiute : An Ethnohistorical View of the Documentary Evidence 1889-1893." *Ethnohistory : the Bulletin of the Ohio Valley Historic Indian Conference* 27(3):267-288(Summer 1980).

Here is an historical, well-documented review of the 1890 Ghost Dance among the Paiutes of Nevada, contrasted with the event in South Dakota. Personal interviews with participants and with the Ghost Dance prophet, Jack Wilson himself give much detailed information. The conclusion to the investigation into why the two movements were so different lies in the different amount of acculturation to which the two significant tribes (the Paiutes in Nevada and the Sioux in South Dakota) had been subject. Nevada newspaper articles are quoted here, demonstrating the awareness of the Ghost Dance celebrations among the whites in the area, and the Agent C.C. Warner is quoted. The government personnel responsible for the Nevada territory "adopted a 'laissez faire' policy toward the religion and local whites maintained attitudes of 'benign neglect' or ridicule." The economic relationship between the whites and Indians in Nevada was interdependent, i.e. the Indians were not dependent on their agencies for their welfare. In South Dakota, however, the Sioux were the "victims of unceasing and merciless cultural [and economic] deprivation." In Nevada, the primary reason for adopting the Ghost Dance was the charisma of the Ghost Dance Messiah, Jack Wilson. In South Dakota, the religion was "embraced because it offered hope."

Appended to this article is the report, dated Dec. 6. 1890, of Mr. A.I. Chapman concerning his interview with Capt. Josephus of the Paiute Indian police, whose interview with and investigation of, Jack Wilson, "the 'personated'[sic] Christ," served to substantiate the then current rumors of the Ghost Dance Messiah and religion.

86.   Lowie, Robert. *Indians of the Plains.* New York, Toronto, London : McGraw-Hill Book Company, 1954.

The culture of the Plains Indians is the subject of this exhaustive study of the Indians found "between the Mississippi River and the Rocky Mountains, along with the adjacent parts of Canada." These tribes are incorporated into six linguistic "families," which include the Algonkian, Athabaskan, Caddoan, Kiowan, Siouan, and the Uto-Aztecan families. These families are divided into 30 distinct tribes.

The cultural study presented here is the available information from the time of "discovery until their virtually complete assimilation of the White man's ways." This includes information on all aspects of the life of the people, -- diet and food preparation, hunting and hunting techniques, agriculture and bartering for food, dwellings, social organization, economic relationships, religion and world beliefs and art.

Lowie deals with the Ghost Dance Movement in his section on *Modern Movements*, which also includes the Peyote Cult. In his discussion of the Ghost Dance Movement, Lowie presents both the 1870 and the 1890 Movement, describing the earlier one, "developed by a Paviotso Indian in Nevada who went into trances and preached that the deceased were about to return to earth and that the ancient life was to be restored along with the game animals then growing scarce." In 1888, the "prophet's younger kinsman, Wovoka" regenerated the movement and, began teaching his followers a dance which was supposed to bring about the return of the dead. He combined his doctrine with "ethical teaching, prohibiting fighting and enjoining peace with the Whites." He combined Christian teachings with pagan ideas, "at one time pretending to be Christ returning to renew the aging earth. This need for renovating the earth is an old and widespread American Indian conception."

The earlier of these two movements was not received by the Plains Indians. However, in 1888 means of communication as well as transportation were improved, so that "interested Indians" from the Plains could travel to Nevada and visit with the prophet. The Teton Dakota, the Arapaho, the Cheyenne and Kiowa "more especially seized on what they supposed to be the new faith, though actually they completely changed its import." "Goaded into fury by their grievances, the disciples of Wovoka in the Plains substituted for his policy of amity, a holy war in which the whites were to be exterminated." As much as possible, elements of the whites were to be "tabooed," while vestiges of the old life were encouraged. "Under the impetus of this cult, hostile demonstrations broke out among the Teton under the leadership of Sitting Bull, who was killed by Indian Police on December 15, 1890. A fortnight later there was a battle at Wounded Knee, where 31 soldiers and 128 Dakota were killed."

In a subsequent chapter, Acculturation, Lowie defines this term as "the changes produced in the cultures of peoples in continuous contact with each other." He continues, "When the two groups differ in complexity, the simpler culture is likely to be more receptive than the other. Such was the relative status of Indians and Caucasians, the latter more frequently playing the donor's role."

87.   Mair, Lucy P. "Independant Religious Movements in Three Continents." *Comparative Studies in Society and History* 1:113-136(1959).

This is a comparative investigation into three aboriginal groups, in three distinct ethnographic areas in the world: Indians of the American Northwest celebrating the Ghost Dance, peoples of the South Pacific in Cargo Cults, and the Bantu of southern and central Africa, involved with the reinterpretation of the Christianity brought to them by missionaries. The religions of these three groups are discussed and compared here.

Mair finds major distinctions between the tenets of these religions, born of the incursion of a dominant cultural group:

1.   The Ghost Dance Movement was based in the desire to escape the white man, and reject everything he had brought with him. The Cargo Cults, on the other hand, desired the material goods, the official titles, the technical expertise, and the power which was in the hands of the dominant group. They were interested in taking the material goods away from the European interlopers. The arrival of the Cargo was prayed for. The toy weapons used in the ceremonies were to have changed into real ones, to be used in the confrontation.

2.   The Ghost Dance Movement was celebrated, by and large by groups who had been forcibly "cut-off from their accustomed way of life." Relocated onto reservations, without their previous food suplies, i.e. buffalo herds decimated, wild game and fish gone, the Ghost Dance was a longing for the return of life in previous times, for the old ways. The Cargo Cults did not experience this severance from their traditional culture, and demonstrated no particular desire for a return of the past.

3.   A key part of the past expected to return to the Ghost Dancers was the population, i.e. their deceased family and friends. The Cargo Cults of the South Pacific, influenced by Christian missionaries, developed myths based on traditional beliefs in combination with Christianity. They were involved in the notion of "the return of the dead," but these were to return as white skinned people. The local natives would, at the same time, *become* white skinned, and somehow, those who were white, would become black.

4.   Both movements developed moral constrictions, at least in part to aid in existing successfully with each other, as well as with the dominant group.

88.   Moses, L.G. "James Mooney and Wovoka: An Ethnologist's Visit with the Ghost Dance Prophet." *Nevada Historical Society Quarterly.* 30(2):131-146(1987).

This article follows the trail of Mooney's life which led him, as a relative novice ethnologist, to seek out the Ghost Dance prophet in Nevada, enlarge on his understanding of the Ghost Dance Movement through the Cheyenne and Arapaho tribes, also involved with the Movement, and finally to publish his findings in his *The Ghost Dance Religion and the Sioux Outbreak of 1890.* Mooney and his superior at the Smithsonian Institution, Bureau of American Ethnology, John Wesley Powell, were among the few interested in this phenomenon. Moses details the sometimes deliberate lack of interest on the part of the Bureau of Indian Affairs and other parts of the U.S. Government, at all levels. C.C. Warner, Superintentent of the Nevada Agencies and the Indian Agent in charge of the Pyramid Lake reservation, Wovoka's home, pursued "a course of non-attention or a silent ignoring" with Wovoka.

Moses also discusses the position Mooney takes in his book that the Ghost Dance Religion was a "universalist" one. Though aboriginal, the religion was "common to the human heart", and "essentially the same" as other major religions in the world, a theme which has generated much controversy. Alternately, Moses suggests that "Mooney wrote as a historian...who sees themes that transcend denomination or particular philosophy, tribe or nation." Mooney's book, Moses suggests, is the "fountainhead of research" on the Ghost Dance of 1890 and its prophet.

89.   Overholt, Thomas. "The Ghost Dance of 1890 and the Nature of the Prophetic Process." *Ethnohistory*, Bulletin of the Ohio Valley Historic Indian Conference. 2(1):37-63(1974).

This is a substantive investigation into the basic nature of the prophetic phenomenon and into the Ghost Dance as such a phenomenon. Overholt suggests a minimum of three components to the prophetic process:

1. Prophet's revelation
2. The message from the revelation needing 3 characteristics -
    a. continuity with cultural traditions
    b. cognizance of current historical situation
    c. adequate account of relevant factors outside of Prophet's culture.

3. Feedback from the people in the form of
   a. action or
   b. a set of expectations.

Compliance with these features is demonstrated and discussed through comments from a selection of Ghost Dance historians. An additional five components are added, which basically incorporate the momentum of the prophetic phenomenon itself, into its own life. This study in fact, uses the Ghost Dance phenomenon to discuss the prophetic process, assuming that the presence of a paradigmatic theory to attach to this movement would provide clear access to the discussion.

90.   Park, Willard Z. "Paviotso Shamanism." *American Anthropologist* n.s.36:98-113(1934).

This inquiry into shamanism among the Paviotso provides an interesting dimension to the study of the Ghost Dance Movement because, even though it was written in 1934, the informants consulted here existed in a tangible relationship with the shaman and had always done so, as had their families. Park mentions, "Many informants expressed a strong opinion that Jack Wilson, or Wovoka, the messiah of the 1890 Ghost Dance Movement, was the last powerful shaman." Park reports that, while "many of the old religious beliefs and practices flourish today among the Paviotso in Nevada,..." there was already in 1934 a sense that the shamans were "no longer as powerful as they were in the old days."

The social position, means of acquiring shamanistic power, specific functions and healing methods used by shamans of the Paviotso (or, as Park indicates, a shaman from another tribe, who was considered just as powerful) are outlined in this work.

There are features key to shamanistic facility which also emerge in the Ghost Dance Movement. A shaman is, often, initially *instructed* in the ways of a shaman by a deceased relative. A shaman's capacity to revive the dead is related from several informants. The likely availablity of connection with the dead seems consistent with the Ghost Dance Movement. Control of the weather is refered to as something only the strongest shamans are able to do. One informant relates: "Jack Wilson could bring rain," and he relates Wilson's ability when he could "summon clouds with the wave of a feather; [and] it began to rain." Then, "Wilson waves the feather and the clouds disperse."   Park explains that this is "the only occasion on which the shaman uses his power purely for purposes of exhibition." However, Park later reports "The shamans with the strongest powers were thought to be invulnerable against bullets or arrows." As with weather control, this power was excercised to demonstrate the strength of the shaman. Frank Spencer, "one of the messiahs of the 1870 Ghost Dance...was supposed to be invulnerable when fired upon with a gun."

91.   Spier, Leslie. *The Prophet Dance of the Northwest and Its Derivatives : The Source of the Ghost Dance.* General Series in Anthropology; University of California. 1:74(1935).

This monographs traces the origin and distribution of the Ghost Dance Movements of 1870 and 1890 and other related movements in the Northwest United States. Spier states his purpose here to be "to show that the ultimate origin of the two Ghost Dance movements was not with the Paviotso but in the Northwest among the tribes of the interior Plateau area. It can be shown that among these peoples there was an old belief in the impending destruction and renewal of the world, when the dead would return, in conjunction with which there was a dance based on supposed imitation of the dances of the dead, and a conviction that intense preoccupation with the dance would hasten the happy day."

Spier includes many individual types of religious celebration, extant before the 1870 Ghost Dance movement in Nevada, under the rubric of the *Prophet Dance,* a term which he coined for reference to similar religious ceremonies found in the "northwestern interior plateau culture area." His investigation includes the Christian missions and churches from the early part of the 19th century in the U.S. and Canada, Messiah cults in the MacKenzie area, the Smohalla cult and the Pom-Pom-Feather religion, as well as the Ghost Dance Movements originating in Nevada in both 1870 and 1980 and their derivatives. All these movements involve relations of the living with the dead. Spier includes all of these movements under the name Prophet Dance.

In this study, Spier draws a detailed picture of exactly how each movement led to or was related to the others, how they were different, and what was original about those that were original.

I would like to draw the reader's attention to another of Spier's works concerning the Ghost Dance, "The Ghost Dance of 1870 Among the

Klamath of Oregon. " *Publications in Anthropology, University of Washington*, 2 (1927).

92.   Strong, William Duncan. "The Occurrence and Wider Implications of a 'Ghost Cult' on the Columbia River Suggested by Carvings in Wood, Bone and Stone." *American Anthropologist* n.s.47:244-261 (1945).

Strong discusses the many examples, recorded over an extensive length of time, of a consistent anthropomorphic type figure found in the Columbia River area in what is now Washington state. The first mention of these figures is quoted from Captain Clark, from the Lewis and Clark expedition. The figures he mentions were wooden, "do not appear to be for adoration" but "as resemblences of those whose decease they indicate; when we observe them in houses, they occupy the most conspicuous part, but are treated more like ornaments than objects of worship."(1805) Strong describes two figures thought to be "of the type described by the early explorers. "The two carved wooden effigies had been inserted in a talus slope close under an overhanging crag and were thus protected from the elements." "Being made of cedar the effigies may well have a considerable antiquity." "They are anthropomorphic, the headdress or hats and the clearly delineated ribs being their most outstanding characteristic." This motif aparently occurs elswhere in the northwest coast region: the Salish wooden figures with accentuated ribs, and "a number of wooden as well as stone, effigies and carved artifacts mostly from the vicinity of The Dallas of the Columbia River, executed in the same or in more elaborate style and often marked ribs."

Strong also describes the discovery of many similar effigies from several other locations along the Columbia River, in either stone, bone or antler as well as petroglyphs. They are marked with clear "skeletal accentuation, particularly rib delineation, which marks the rarer wooden carvings preserved from the same region."

There follows a discussion of the decimation of the Indians in this area, cause unknown, in a very short time. Lewis and Clark, in 1805 noted many abandoned villages and many evidences of contact with whites [e.g. gonorrhea and syphilis] by way of the Pacific. Just nine years later in 1814, another trader noted the prevalence of these diseases that had occurred after 1810 (the date white traders established a post at the mouth of the Columbia River).

In any case, "...in the greater northwest, ethno-historical analysis clearly indicates the early and wide spread evidence of a Prophet Dance concerned with death and revival, long anterior but ancestral to the later well-known Ghost Dances." Strong cites a recurrent theme in Northwest Coast mythology, that of "visits of the living with the dead. Many of these recount purely mythical adventures but quite as frequently they are couched in historical happenings." It is also discovered that at the southern end of this region, premature burial was "not uncommon" and therefore not surprisingly, people who had *died,* "returned," in precise parallel to the Plateau prophets.

93.   Thornton, Russell. *American Indian Holocaust and Survival : A Population History Since 1492.* Norman, London : University of Oklahoma Press, 1987.

This is a demographic history of the Indians in North America north of Mexico, from the time of the arrival of Columbus to the present. Thornton describes the consequences for the Indian, of the arrival of the white man, and traces the effect of this contact on the Indian population during the next four centuries. The over all effect was disasterous, "a demographic collapse" of Indian culture and life. The long term patterns used to accomplish this effect are shown to be: "disease, including alcoholism; warfare and genocide; geographical removal and relocation; and destruction of ways of life."

Thornton discusses, in his chapter called "The Ghost Dances," both the movements of 1870 and 1890. The logic for including this discussion in this population history, lies in the fact that they were both "brought about, more or less, directly by the depopulation of the Indians. More important, both of these movements were deliberate efforts to confront, even reverse, the demographic collapse that the Indians had experienced by the late nineteenth century."

Thornton first elaborates on the Ghost Dance of 1870, relating its origin, with the Paviotso, Wodziwob, his initial trance and the message he brought from it. This message was that the dead would return to the earth and make it, once again, into a paradise. Eternal life for the Indians and the disappearance of the white man was also promised. Among Wodziwob's disciples were two fellow Northern Paiutes, Weneyuga (Frank Spencer), and Tavio (or Numataivo), the latter being the father of Wovoka, the prophet of the 1890 Ghost Dance. As the disciples and others spread the religion, new tribes adapted the original message to their own circumstances and beliefs. A common new prophecy involved the return of an "abundance of the animals, fish, and flora on which the American Indian had depended for food." Another common new prophecy dealt with the elimination of non-indians. Yet another was concerned with the exact method by which the dead would return. The dance used was derived from the existing Paviotso ceremonial dance. This was also adapted as the movement grew from tribe to tribe. After 1871, this movement grew even stronger as it spread through California, up the San Joaquin Valley and into Oregon. "One dance in Tulare County, California, was said to have drawn 5,000 to 6,000 Indians from different tribes; as many as 762 of them danced at any one time." Thornton lists, by name, 45 individual tribes which participated in this Ghost Dance Movement or one of its off-shoots, e.g. the Earth Lodge Cult, the Bole-Maru Cult or the Big Head Cult. The ceremonies, songs and dances are described.

The 1890 Ghost Dance is also depicted in depth. Its prophet, Wovoka (The Cutter) was the son of Tavivo, the disciple of Wodziwob. He was probably a teenager at the time of the 1870 movement. His revelation came during an eclipse of the sun. The main tenets of this movement were, like the one in 1870, the return of the dead, a paradise with the animals and food, and the disappearance of non-whites. And as with the 1870 movement, variations began to occur as the movement spread. However, the main concept remained the same. Wovoka, more actively than did Wodziwob, began to spread this movement. James Mooney, (1896), collected many of the songs used in these ceremomies, and some of them, from various tribes, are included here.

Thornton focuses on a brief tribal history of the Sioux. By the 1700's, they had located in the prairies. They had acquired access to horses, and had risen to control of the area from "Minnesota to the Rocky Mountains, and from the Yellowstone to the Platte." In this settting, the Sioux had become thoroughly dependent on the buffalo, for "food, clothing, shelter, social and cultural activities." This was the position of the Sioux at initial contact with the "immigrant white population."

By 1870, due to the nature of the relationship which developed between this white population and the Sioux, several treaties had been signed through which the Sioux retained, for themselves, only reservation land. In 1889, yet another treaty greatly reduced the little land they had left. The buffalo was nearly wiped out. Simultaneously, they were suffering crop "failures, massive disease, population losses in the tribe and in their cattle. An unexpcted cut in their rations from the government left the Sioux starving, and totally dependent on the govenment for support." The government did not support them.

The Sioux participation in the 1889-1890 Ghost Dance is reconstructed, with the Sioux adaptations, which "because of chronic dissatisfaction, ...the movement assumed a hostile expression among the Sioux," (Mooney,1896) in which the Ghost Dance Shirt took on even more importance. The death of Sitting Bull, the panic of the settlers and the resultant military presence in this area are detailed. The Wounded Knee Massacre is described in depth.

Thornton concludes, with a review of the evidence that both Ghost Dances were not, as some scholars have characterized them, movements of *mass hysteria*, but "deliberate religious efforts to confront their dire situations." He also observes that the Ghost Dance was "congruent to the Sioux knowledge system of cause and effect, since religion and science were one and the same to them."

94.   Thornton, Russell. "Demographic Antecedents of a Revitalization Movement: Population Change, Population Size, and the 1890 Ghost Dance." *American Sociological Review* 46:88-96(1981).

Thornton reviews the various ways in which studies of both of the Ghost Dance Movements among the American Indians have been approached: historically with other similar American Indian dances in a "sequence of evolution and/or diffusion; as a response to social and cultural deprivation; as a result of a psychological prophet or messiah; as a revitilization movement or as an instance of religious movements in response to colonialism." He points out that the relationship between the Ghost Dance and the destruction of the American Indian population had been suggested but not studied.

His study begins with the heading: "The Ghost Dance As Demographic Revitalization." In this section, he points out that "...even the name by which it was commonly known among both Indians and whites, 'Spirit' or 'Ghost' Dance referred specifically to the resurrection of the Indians' ancestors by returning "...the spirits of the dead from the spirit world..."(Mooney, 1896:791). He then points to the population size of the American Indian in 1800 at 600,000. This number was reduced to 228,000 by 1890, through "disease, relocation, starvation, genocide, social and cultural destruction." This population decrease was worse for the tribes which were, or would be west of the Mississippi River.

Thornton's reasoning in formulating his study was as follows: "...the objective of the Ghost Dance and historic timing suggest that the Movement was, at least in part, an attempted demographic revitalization to recover population losses. (The recovery would then lead to the renewal of Indian societies and cultures, and the consequent assurance of tribal survival.)" Tribal participation would depend on the tribe's population characteristics relating to size, and especially "changes in size prior to, and absolute size at the time of the Dance." "Tribes experiencing severe population declines would have been more threatened than tribes experiencing only moderate declines or even increases. Similarly, smaller tribes would perhaps have been more threatened than larger ones."

To begin his study, Thorton consulted three sources to determine tribal participation and non-participation: 1. Mooney's (1896) report on the 1890 Ghost Dance, 2. Other anthropological discussions of the movement, and 3. Individual studies and work on acceptance by other anthropologists. Thornton does not include sub-tribal distinctions, and includes 70 tribes which "knew of the Dance; 45 participated in it, 25 did not participate.

The documentation of his population figures is outlined, citing previously published anthropological and ethnological studies, and the U.S. Bureau of the Census.

Thornton ultimately sets up seven possible combinations of data to align, reflecting population and participation in the Ghost Dance. These reflect the relationship between 1) participation and tribal population change between the 1870's and the 1890's; 2) participation and population change from first extensive European contact and 1890; 3) participation and population size in 1890 (i.e. large and small); 4) participation and population change between 1870's and 1890's by 1890 population size; 5) participation and population decline from first extensive European contact to 1890's by 1890 population size; 6) participation and date of first extensive European contact; and 7) participation and date of first extensive European contact with respect to population size in 1890.

Thornton concludes that Ghost Dance participation among small tribes, "especially those with population declines, have been almost total." Further, "Size also influences the relationships between population change and participation (as well as the effects of length of extensive European contact on participation.)"

95.   Thornton, Russell. *We Shall Live Again : The 1870 and 1890 Ghost Dance Movements As Demographic Revitilization.* Cambridge : Cambridge University Press, 1986.

A discussion and demographic description of the Ghost Dance movements of 1870 and 1890 is followed by in-depth scholarly research into the demographic revitalization which resulted from the movements.

Thornton's position, in contrast to previous scholarship on this issue, is that both Ghost Dance Movements (1870 and 1890) were "deliberate attempts to respond to a threatening situation rather than a phenomenon of mass hysteria."

Statistical tables are used of tribe sizes, described in terms of pre-European contact, early 1800's, 1870, 1990, 1910 and 1920. They are matched against tables listing Ghost Dance participation and non-participation.

The demograpic implications available from these statistics are tribe specific. Thornton outlines the socio-cultural differences of each tribe, along with their historical backgrounds.

The evidence offered in Thornton's work demonstrates the overall success of the revitalization aspects of the Ghost Dance Movements in terms of the subsequent size in the 20th century, of the participating tribes and those not participating.

96.   Wallace, Anthony F.C. "Revitalization Movements" *American Anthropologist* 58:264-281(1956).

Wallace has written what has become the definitive investigation into *revitalization*, the phenomenon of "attempted and sometimes successful innovation of whole cultural systems, or at least substantial portions of such systems." After reviewing the various approaches taken by behavioral scientists in the study of these systems, he proposes to use the term *revitalization* in referring to "these phenomena of major cultural-system innovation."

Wallace defines a revitalization movement as "a deliberate, organized, conscious effort by members of a society to construct a more satisfying culture." He then reviews the cultural traits necessary for a given culture to feel the need for revitalization. His discussion here also involves the notion of each individual in a society needing revitalizing. Here he introduces the concept of a "mazeway," reflecting a composite personal-cultural environment, or a "model of the cell-body-personality-nature-culture-society system or field, organized by the individual's own experience" including "perceptions of both the maze of physical objects of the environment (internal and external, human and non-human) and also of the ways in which this maze can be manipulated by the self and others in order to minimize stress." The *real* system may also have to be changed in order to bring *reality* and the "mazeway" into congruence, and "to permit more effective stress reduction..... The collaboration of a number of persons in such an effort is called a *Revitalization Movement.*"

Wallace then outlines this "processual structure" to be composed of five stages: "1. Steady state. 2. Period of individual stress. 3. Period of cultural distortion. 4. Period of revitalization (in which occurs a period of mazeway re-formulation, ...) and 5. New steady state. The period of mazeway reformulation is subsequently enlarged upon.

Other terms indicating other considerations are reviewed as "subclasses with a miscellany of criteria." These include, Nativistic movements, Revivalistic movements, Cargo cults, Vitalistic movements, Millenarian movements, and Messianic movements.

With this article, Wallace has delineated the parameters within which subsequent anthropologists and ethnographers have pursued the study of rapid cultural change.

6

Ghost Dance Music
and Photographs

97. Colby, Leonard Wright, General. "Wanagi Olowan Kin (The Ghost Songs Of The Dakotas.)" *Proceedings and Collections. Nebraska State Historical Society ; Historical Papers [Second Series].* 1(3) January 1, 1895. Lincoln, Nebraska.

This article contains several first hand accounts of Indian visits to the *messiah*, the Ghost Dance prophet. The U.S. War Department circulated a report concerning a Cheyenne named Porcuine who, accompanied by several other Indians from other tribes, had gone to the Walker River Reservation, where they all met the messiah. The agent for the Cheyenne and Araphaho in Oklahoma reported to the Indian Bureau rumors from the Shoshoni, that their best medicine men had visited with the messiah. The agent in charge of the Tongue River Agency reported that an Indian, also named Porcupine, had declared himself the messiah and had a large following. The Sioux from Nebraska and North and South Dakota sent four representatives to Nevada to investigate the rumors. Good Thunder, Cloud Horse, Yellow Knife and Short Bull returned after several months, having talked with the "Indian Christ" and after receiving 1) the necessary instruction for the Dance for their salvation and 2) the paints to use to make them immortal. He told them to follow his instructions and by the next spring, all would be well. Agent Gallagher at the Pine Ridge Agency in South Dakota and Agent McLaughlin at the Standing Rock Agency both reported that groups were participating in the Ghost Dance celebrations in great number.

Colby attempts to clarify with what could be a definitive version of what the Ghost Dance was by presenting "the story of Ghost Dancing" as written out by a young educated Oglala, Major George Sword, then Captain of the Indian police at Pine Ridge. This description includes nineteen stanzas from Ghost Dance songs, in both the original language and translated to English, as well as one complete song, with score and verse, also translated into English.

98.   Grabill, John C.H. "Photographs of the Last Conflict Between the Sioux and the U.S. Military 1890-1891." *South Dakota History* 14(3):222-237(1984)

John C.H. Grabill was an independent photographer who opened his studio in Sturgis, Dakota Territory in 1886, and proceeded to take photographs of military life, Indians, ranching scenes, mining towns and railroad construction. Some of his photographs were taken in Wyoming and Colorado, but his major "focus was on the Black Hills and the Plains to the east."

This small collection is quite memorable, and demonstrates his on-going interest in the Indian life of the time. He was not present at the Battle of Wounded Knee, but some of these photographs were taken shortly thereafter. Also, he had previously recorded scenes at Big Foot's village on the Cheyenne River reservation. Some of these photographs, along with their captions, discreetly touch the heart of the matter. A photograph of the Hotchkiss guns and the men who manned them is titled "Famous Battery 'E' of 1st Artillery." Two pictures of the remnants of the Indian village, each with several Indians, are both titled "What's left of Big Foot's Band." A panoramic view of "The Great Hostile Camp," the Sioux village near Pine Ridge Agency allows the viewer to sense the size of the Ghost Dancers' village, which covered "nearly three miles on both sides of White Clay Creek."

The photographs in this article are quite intimate and moving. The majority of Grabill's original photographs are in the Prints and Photographs Division of the Library of Congress.

99.   Hamilton, Henry W. *The Sioux of the Rosebud : A History In Pictures.* Photographs by John A. Anderson; text by Henry and Jean Tyree Hamilton. Norman : University of Oklahoma Press, 1971.

This is a collection of 243 photographs taken in the still very wild West, of a cross section of the population, including Sioux Indians. The pictures are of families, individuals, tribal portraits, individual portraits, Ghost Dances, Ghost Dancers and other dancers. Also included are military personnel, military camps, cowboy round-ups, school buildings and celebrations.

This book is a very satisfying pictorial history of those lives. The accompanying text provides an excellent background for this intimate view of the Nebraska and South Dakota plains in the last decades of the 19th century.

100.   Herzog, George. "Plains Ghost Dance and Great Basin Music." *American Anthropologist.* n.s.37 (1935).

This is an inquiry into the relationship betwen the music from the Great Basin and that from the Great Plains. The musical style in general, of the Indians from the Great Basin, is foreign to that of the Plains Indians. Nevertheless, this music from the Great Basin penetrated the Plains in the form of the Ghost Dance.

Herzog examines all Ghost Dance melodies available to him -- thirty-eight -- and finds a surprising uniformity in them.

The linguistic investigation into the texts or lyrics of the songs was not determined germane to Herzog's study, and was not dealt with separately.

The analysis is condensed into tabular form and is arranged to offer comparison, tribal group to tribal group. Those tribes included are Arapaho, Pawnee, Caddo, Kiowa, Comanche, Teton Dakota Sioux and Yankton Dakota Sioux.

101.   Highwater, Jamake. *Ritual of the Wind : North American Indian Ceremonies, Music and Dances*. New York Viking Press, 1977.

This book reviews Indian dances and ceremonies of different tribes, performed in the past and today, along with an explanation of their meanings. The discussion of the social and religious continuity available through these celebrations is documented and well supported with the use of many photographs -- some from the 19th century, some contemporary.

Highwater deals with the Ghost Dance in several places as the point after which "They would not rise again." He describes Sitting Bull's death, the incident at Wounded Knee Creek, Big Foot's death and the military aspect of the confrontation. The point he makes in the book in general, however, is the indisputable survival of Indians and Indian culture in North America, in spite of everything done to the contrary.

102.   La Farge, Oliver. *A Pictorial History of the American Indian*. by Oliver La Farge, revised by Alvin M. Josephy, Jr. New York : Bonanza Books, 1966, 1974.

This is an entertaining book, in a large (31x24 cm.) format, filled with illustrations, drawings, photographs of individuals, groups, clothing, art, artifacts, dwellings and religions paraphernalia of tribes of Indians in North America.

Included is a three page article concerning "Ghosts and Drugs", a discussion of the options left most of the Indians in the late 19th century, and the direction many of them have taken. La Farge discusses the Ghost Dance as "directly a result of Christian mission influence", originating in Nevada with Wovoka, in about 1888. Wovoka's religion combined Christian ethical ideas and the notion of a coming messiah with rituals designed to make the white man disappear, the buffalo return and the old ways of the Indian once again available. Wovoka's message was one of peace, living the *right* way and getting along with the whites until such time as they would be, non-violently, removed.

The Sioux pilgrims, arriving from South Dakota to inquire about this religion, received the notion of the peaceful celebration of the Ghost Dance. However when they returned home with the instuctions, the explanation of the Ghost Dance whch they related to their people was much more aggressive than the one which they had originally received.

This article includes a photograph of Wovoka, and paintings of an Oglala Sioux Ghost Dance, an Arapaho Ghost Dance, a photograph of a moment in the Arapaho Ghost Dance ritual and a photograph of an Arapaho Ghost Dance Shirt.

103. Scherer, Joanna Cohan. *Indians : The Great Photographs That Reveal North American Indian Life, 1847-1929, from the Unique Collection of the Smithsonian Institution.* New York : Crown, 1973.

This is a valuable collection of photographs of high quality which are germane, ethnographically, to our subject. They are divided into three sections: 1) The way they looked; 2) The way they lived; and 3) Envoys to Washington.

The photographs range from individual portraits, to family portraits, to tribal portaits. These include two pictures of an Arapaho Ghost Dance, in process, taken by James Mooney in 1893 in the Oklahoma territory.

104. Vander, Judith. *Ghost Dance Songs and Religion of a Wind River Shoshone Woman.* Los Angeles, California : University of California Press, 1987. Monograph Series in Ethnomusicology no. 4, Program in Ethnomusicology, Department of Music.

Vander has culled the information for this book through lengthy interviews with two Shoshoni women who were half-sisters: Emily Hill and Dorothy Tappay. She has included here 17 Shoshone Ghost Dance songs, which she has analyzed both musically and textually, to define the musical and poetic style.

Dorothy Tappay made tapes of the songs over the years and Vander was able to refer to her tapes for this study. The two women, orphaned and widowed, living together, continued to participate in the Ghost Dance ceremonies, which continue to be practiced today among their tribe in Wyoming. The Shoshone culture has a closer relationship to other cultures in the Great Basin than to those in the Great Plains, and so the strong connection to the Ghost Dance remains.

105.   Vennum, Thomas, Jr. "Music" , *Handbook of North American Indians*.
       11:682-704(1986).

This article is an inquiry into the Native American tribes and their
music. A lengthy section discusses the musical aspects of the Ghost
Dance, as well as the choreography therein. Vennum discusses the
nature of the music in the Nevada Ghost Dance ceremonies conducted
by Wovoka, much of the content original with him. Vennum traces how
this music changed as it spread to the Northeast.

7
Government and
Military Histories

106. Feaver, Eric. "Indian Soldiers, 1891-1895: An Experiment on the Closing Frontier." *Prologue : The Journal of the National Archives.* 7(2):109-118(1975).

The experiment referred to in the title was one of enlisting Indians, all across the country, into the United States army. After a brief review of the general concept and history of the Ghost Dance Movement, including the events at Wounded Knee Creek, Feaver begins to recount the generally unsuccessful attempt to recruit "Indian braves" into the U.S. army. In January 1891, less than a month after the Battle of Wounded Knee, the commanding general of the United States army, John M. Schofield, suggested to the Secretary of War, Redfield Proctor, that "2000 young Indians be enlisted in the army...." "He believed such action would stabilize Indian reservations by providing restless, dissatisfied braves with useful employment and would help mold the Indians from savages into civilized, responsible American citizens."

Feaver suggests several possible features in this rationale: "If it could enlist dissident Sioux, it might quench the Ghost Dance Movement." Also,"Schofield thought the Indians would welcome the oportunity to be soldiers. He believed that 'there is in their [the Sioux] mind no employment [more] worthy of an Indian brave than that of a soldier.'" In addition, the feeling among military personnel was that the army should "exert military control over the recalcitrant Indians in peacetime, as well as in emergencies that the Indian Bureau seemed unable to handle." The jealous relationship between the Department of War and the Department of the Interior, with its control of the Indian Bureau seems to have played a part in the military's pursuit of this idea. "Army bureaucrats", it is suggested, felt the assimilation of the Indians would be better handled by them than by the Indian Bureau.

In February, 1891, officers traveled throughout the Sioux territory, attempting to enlist recruits for five year enlistments, in California. Not one Indian decided to join. Unwilling to leave their families and "their ponies" for such a long time, they preferred to stay at home, and enlist, for better wages and for six months, as scouts. The Federal Government decided to broaden the recruitment effort to all Indians, and to drastically reduce the number of Indian scouts. "Recruiting officers scoured the west for recruits." By February, 1892, there were five cavalry and six infantry units "more or less at full strength," and six infantry units were nearing completion. In 1891, the number of Indians enlisted was 759. Some the the major tribes showed absolutely no interest. Several humorous incidents are recounted, involving recruiting officers crossing paths with 1) other military groups investigating the "Messiah craze," thus alienating the possible recruits; and with 2) a "representative of the Smithsonian Institute [in the area] to measure Indian faces and forms with instruments hardly intended to quiet the fears of suspicious and ignorant Indians."

Among the Indians who did enlist, life was not good. Liquor became a major problem. The question of authority arose, within the army, between the army and the Indian Bureau, and between the army and local peace officials. Ultimately, Feaver states: "The attempt to make citizens of warriors failed...."

107. "Messiah War On The Cheyenne River" *Wi-Ty-Ohi* Bulletin of the South Dakota Historical Society 16(8) November, 1963.

This work affords us a day by day reconstruction of the movements of Sitting Bull and his friend and co-leader/Chief, Big Foot, between July and December in 1890. We also trace the military orders conveyed to the various troops, theoretically to ensure the safety of the whites in the area from the Sioux. The massive increase in the troops, requested by D.F. Royer, newly appointed Agent at Pine Ridge, was supplied by General Nelson A. Miles.

James McLaughlin, Agent at Standing Rock Agency, and his part in the attempted arrest of Chief Sitting Bull, the death of that Chief, and the escape of Big Foot along with the rest of Sitting Bull's band are among the events related.

Erroneous communication between U.S. military personnel and between them and white settlers, some of whom felt they had nothing to fear, and the illness and subsequent paranoia of Big Foot are all shown to have contributed to the needless Wounded Knee Massacre.

This article is compiled from contemporary newspapers and U.S. government reports. A good map is included.

108.   Moses, L.G. "Jack Wilson and the Indian Service: the Response of the BIA to the Ghost Dance Prophet." *American Indian Quarterly* 5(4):295-316(1979).

This article seeks verification of some kind of awareness on the part of the Bureau of Indian Affairs regarding the Ghost Dance Movement, its impact on the tribes it involved, even of the identity of its prophet.

Letters of concern over the increasing interest in the Movement sent to local Indian Agents, and to the Acting Commissioner of Indian Affairs are cited. The letters are discovered to have had little or no response.

Responsibility for the relatively oblivious state in which the Bureau of Indian Affairs found itself in 1891 is found in several areas. The Nevada Indian Agents were in a position to have investigated Wovoka and his message. They did not. Rivalry for control of Indian Affairs between the Bureau of Indian Affairs and the War Department might have had a counterproductive effect on the exchange of helpful information.

Ultimately, Moses laments "...the uncompromising indifference, in ways the greater tragedy, of those persons entrusted with the administration of Indian affairs...."

109.   Welsh, Herbert. "The Meaning of the Dakota Outbreak." *Scribner's Magazine*. April, 1891. (p.439-452.)

A review of President Grant's Peace Policy and his appointment of the Board of Indian Commissioners, is followed by an acknowledgment of the widespread corruption and dishonesty in the supposed service to the Indian. This is the overall thrust of this article. With the exception of a few remarkable men like Dr. Valentine McGillycuddy, Agent, Pine Ridge Agency and James McLaughlin, Agent, Standing Rock Agency, the system of agency appointments was based on the Spoils System. These positions, which were so important to the smooth administration of the recently established Indian reservations, were awarded, not necessarily to the brightest, most honest, most conscientious, not even the most experienced. These positions were awarded to friends or political connections of the President, Secretary of the Interior, or the Commissioner of Indian Affairs.

Welsh details how this practice exacerbated the tenuous situation in South Dakota in 1890, leading to the Wounded Knee Massacre.

110.   Wooster, Robert. *The Military and United States Indian Policy, 1865-1903.* New Haven and London : Yale University Press, 1988.

This is a narrative of the subject, carefully documented by military records and correspondence concerning the events related. The author, of course, has the hindsight of the historian on his side. His narrative, however, is quite objective, and so, insightful and interesting.

He deals with the Ghost Dance phenomenon in his chapter called "Twilight of the Old Army, 1877-1903". Some of the military personnel in the Dakotas felt the military build-up was not necessary and finally counter-productive. There were also other messages and demands for protection. With Brig. Gen. Thomas H. Ruger, of the Department of Dakota, and Brig. Gen. John Brooke, of the Department of the Platte, and with the military orchestration of General Nelson A. Miles, the troops were indeed amassed.

It is related that Big Foot's band of Miniconjou, "fearful of white betrayal," and rallied by the medicine man, Yellow Bird, refused to cooperate with Col. Forsyth's Seventh Cavalry, and, tensions being what they were by that time, the Wounded Knee Massacre ensued.

The available detail of these events in this well documented narrative is satisfying and unique in its military perspective.

Author Index

Journal Index

Subject Index

About the Compiler

SHELLEY ANNE OSTERREICH is Assistant Librarian at Central Connecticut State University.